Reign of Terror

Leo Silva

Edge Weaver LLC

Reign of Terror

Odyssey is an imprint of Edge Weaver LLC

Book Design: Marie Pitrat

Kindle ISBN: 978-1-964406-40-4

Paperback ISBN: 978-1-964406-41-1

Hardcover ISBN: 978-1-964406-50-3

Published in the United States of America

Edge Weaver LLC
19360 Rinaldi #681
Porter Ranch, CA 91326-1607

Disclaimer

The events and characters in this book are true to the best of the author's knowledge. However, names, places, and events may have been changed or fictionalized for the purposes of privacy and narrative coherence. The intent of this book is to provide an accurate portrayal of the cases and individuals involved, but readers should be aware that it is based on available information, which may be incomplete or subject to interpretation.

The author and publisher have made every effort to ensure the accuracy and completeness of the content. However, they assume no responsibility for errors or omissions. This book is not intended to serve as legal advice or a comprehensive account of the cases discussed.

The opinions expressed in this book are those of the author and do not necessarily reflect the views of the publisher. The publisher does not endorse or assume responsibility for the views expressed by the author.

Dedication and Praise for Reign of Terror

Dedicated to the memory of my mentor and confidante, Mario L. Alvarez. Thank you for your guidance and all your teachings both on and off the job.

To my second mentor, Robert L. Brightwell aka: "Bobby" aka: "Bad Dope" thank you for inspiring me to endeavor to always be the best that I can be, no matter the circumstances.

To Tony Tamayo, thank you for believing in me and introducing me to the world of Law Enforcement. Nothing that is in this book would be possible if it weren't for you.

To my best friend Christopher "the Pole" Polanco. Thank you for being there through thick and thin, good times and bad, happiness and grief. Rest in peace my friend.

Above all to my little brother, Angel Luis Collazo, your spirit will forever serve as the wind beneath my wings. Love you little brother. Till we meet again.

"In *Reign of Terror*, Leo Silva masterfully recounts the rise and fall of the notorious and ultra-violent Los Zetas cartel. But more than just retelling the story, Leo's work is filled with inside information and insights that bring the reader into the world of those tasked with dismantling Los Zetas. Compelling, Leo brings profound humanity to the fight against the Zetas, a fight that brought both victories and tragedies, all of which are deeply felt by the reader."

Jack Luellen, Author of *Someone Had to Die*
Podcast Host: "Cartels, Conspiracies and Camarena"

"*Reign of Terror* takes you on an educational and unique internal view of the DEA combating the Northeast Mexican Cartels, especially the Zetas. Special Agent Leo Silva shares firsthand knowledge of this ongoing war in this page turner. A must read!"

Victor Avila, Former ICE Supervisory Special Agent and author of *Agent Under Fire*

"*Reign of Terror* by Leo Silva brings the Mexican drug war to life. His descriptions of characters and events, along with his experience as a DEA Special Agent working in Mexico, makes you feel like the drug war is happening around you. The book details the rise of Los Zeta's in northern Mexico and how they expanded throughout Mexico and internationally. I'd highly recommend this book for anyone who likes true crime, but it's a MUST READ for those with an interest in the D.E.A., International Drug Cartels, or how complex international crime can be."

Doug Lamplugh, Retired DEA Supervisor and Author of *Murder at Mardi Gras*

"Even though I walk through the valley of the shadow of death, I will fear no evil, for you are with me; thy rod and thy staff comfort me."
(Psalm 23:4)

Contents

Prologue   1

Chapter 1: Hometown   3

Chapter 2: History of DEA and its Role in Mexico   13

Chapter 3: "El Puma"   23

Chapter 4: "El Canicon"   55

Chapter 5: "El Amarillo"   79

Chapter 6: "El Hummer"   89

Chapter 7: Rocking and Rolling   95

Chapter 8: Justice   103

Chapter 9: Another Trifecta   117

Chapter 10: Vortex of Corruption   133

Chapter 11: Follow the Money - The Hunt for "El Rambo"   147

Chapter 12: Shark Hunt   161

Chapter 13: Game Changer   175

Chapter 14: 2011 Agents Down   195

Chapter 15: The Worst Day   219

Chapter 16: Casino Royale   233

Chapter 17: Nowhere to Run   247

Epilogue   253

All About the Author   257

Prologue

I have a story to tell. I cordially invite you to follow me as I lead you on a journey through the mysteriously infernal and bone-chilling world of Cartel warfare in Mexico, where evil thrives and where men and women with no hearts or souls operate with impunity. Along the way, I want to share with you the grief, excitement, pain, and anger that my colleagues in the Drug Enforcement Administration and I endured during our time fighting the Gulf cartel and Zetas in Monterrey Nuevo Leon, Mexico. It was an extremely challenging yet rewarding time for many of us down there. I hope this story enlightens you to the challenges faced by US Drug Enforcement agents stationed in Mexico and many other countries worldwide. I also hope this story enlightens you about the dark, brutal, and malevolent world of drug traffickers. Although this may not be the most extraordinary story about the DEA or its agents, it is mine, and I'd like to tell you if you will listen. Some stories may seem unfathomable, but they are authentic, save for some name changes for safety reasons. In telling you this story, I will relive some painful moments in my life, but I must tell it, before time and the human body's self-defense mechanism erases it from my brain forever. So be my guest as I welcome you into this dark underworld, where the sights are haunting and the atmosphere is suffocating, a shadowy, parallel world that exists alongside ours. Feel the pain with me, shed the tears with me, laugh at the good times with me, curse Satan with me, and, if nothing else, listen to me and believe me.

Chapter 1: Hometown

I grew up in a small, historic, and beautiful town near the sea, known as Brownsville, Texas, which is separated from Matamoros, Mexico by the Rio Grande River. The river flows from South Central Colorado to the Gulf of Mexico and serves as a natural boundary between the United States and Mexico, where Brownsville and Matamoros coexist. The Texas Gulf coastal land flows from South Padre Island to Port Arthur in east Texas. On the Mexican side, it stretches south from Matamoros to the Mexican state of Quintana Roo. The Rio Grande Valley encompasses the entire area from Brownsville to Roma, TX, which is situated eighty miles west of Brownsville. In my humble—and admittedly biased—opinion, Brownsville has arguably the richest history of any Valley city, having served as a major Confederate stronghold during the Civil War. Fort Brown, headquartered in Brownsville, Texas, was a crucial and strategic fort during the Civil War because of its proximity to Mexico, facilitating the smuggling of Confederate goods into Mexico to European ships docked on the Mexican Gulf coast.

Aside from its historic importance, Brownsville is a beautiful city surrounded by freshwater lakes, a mixture of bright, colorful tropical foliage, rare birds, the nearby coastal waters of the Gulf, and, of course, Mexico. My family came from humble beginnings, like many families in the United States. My siblings and I enjoyed a happy childhood. As kids, in 1974, we didn't know what we didn't know. We didn't know that my mom, a single mom, struggled to put food on the table; we didn't know that the divorce from our father caused her an infinite amount of grief, pain, anxiety, and overwhelming financial burdens. But she was a strong, resourceful woman and found respite in the beauty of the Gulf Coast city known as South Padre Island. The island was a stone's throw from Brownsville, and we visited often. It was not uncommon for my mom to spontaneously pack up a bunch of clothes, towels, and sandwiches, load my sister, brother and me into the car and head for the beach, which served as our playground. Utterly oblivious to our mom's silent suffering, we played in the surf, built sandcastles, searched for the ever-elusive sand dollars, fished, hunted for unique-looking shells, tiny hermit crabs, clams, mullet, or just frolicked happily in the refreshing saltwater surf of the Gulf of Mexico.

In retrospect, as much as she wanted to see me and my siblings happy, the trips to the island were therapeutic for her and brought her peace, tranquility, and much-needed escape from the cruel realities of a single mom's life in 1974. For the cost of a tank of gasoline and whatever soft drinks, chips, a loaf of bread, and bologna cost in 1974, we had the time of our lives. With our bellies full of bologna sandwiches and potato chips, we couldn't resist teasing the seagulls, by tossing chips as high as we could into the sky, thrilled to see them up close as they dove for the chips we tossed to them, their shrill laughter blending with our own before we finally had to head home. Reality set in as we drove across the South Padre Island causeway as Elton John's "Don't Let the Sun Go Down on Me" played softly on AM radio. As we drove across the causeway, God treated us to a canvas of the most unforgettably breathtaking mixture of pink, blue, orange, and gray meshed sunsets, whose reflection off the Laguna Madre, resembled a shimmering, golden paradise, beckoning us to return soon. The song made my young heart yearn to stay in those happy moments and never return to Brownsville. I hoped desperately that the sun would never go down and keep us on the beaches in perpetual happiness.

Sunburned and exhausted, with the odor of seawater permeating every pore of our hair and skin, we returned to our home in Brownsville to face the cruel realities of life that most kids face such as school, chores, and neighborhood bullies, far removed from the wonderful beach life we had discovered and loved. In my young, innocent mind, Brownsville was a peacefully idyllic little town where my friends and I played baseball, football, and golf, raced on our bikes and skateboards, hunted white-winged doves, rabbits, squirrels, and lizards long after sunset and well into the evening. After coming home drenched in sweat and covered in dirt, my grandparents had supper waiting, which comprised of arroz con pollo (chicken and rice), a side of refried beans, and a stack of freshly made, steaming hot flour tortillas—not a fancy meal. Still, we felt like royalty, and I'd give anything to have and enjoy that dish today. Of course, I can buy this dish at any Mexican restaurant worth its salt, but it won't ever have the magical touch that my grandparents applied whenever they prepared this dish for me and my siblings. Not even close.

After supper and after showering off the grime from the day's adventures, bedtime came. I usually stayed overnight with my grandparents because school was walking distance for me. My grandparents' house sat directly in front of the railroad tracks, and most times, in the wee morning hours, the train came rumbling by, shaking the entire house as if an earthquake had struck, it appeared the conductor would blow the train's whistle right as the engine passed by our house. But neither the train nor the whistle bothered me. They actually soothed and comforted me and gave me a sense of security, in that all was well in our little world in Brownsville, Texas. To this day, whenever I hear the train's whistle in the wee early morning hours, in the comfort of my home, I am projected back in time to those treasured moments in the sanctum of my grandparents' house, when life was simple, innocent, and wholesome. I had no idea what the Drug Enforcement Administration (DEA) was or what narcotics were, for that matter. I did not know that right across the Rio Grande River from Brownsville in the Mexican city of Matamoros, Tamaulipas, a sinister and dark underworld existed; The predecessor of what is now the Gulf Cartel, thrived off the drug trade and other illicit activities that organized crime usually perpetuates, such as prostitution, gambling, extortion, murder for hire, kidnappings, and bribery of high-level public officials both in the United States and Mexico. I didn't know what I didn't know.

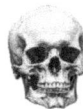

Crime, especially smuggling contraband, is a recurring theme in music (narco-corridos), Mexican television shows (novellas), literature, and daily news in the Rio Grande Valley. Narco-corridos are Mexican folk ballads that tell a story and glorify the protagonist, although mostly the protagonist has a character flaw related to smuggling narcotics, gambling or infidelity, or a combination of all three. This recurring theme is embedded in the Mexican culture and is a part of everyday life in the Rio Grande Valley. Many young men in the Valley aspire to be like the characters glorified in narco-corridos, who live dangerous but apparent glamorous lives, surrounded by guns, drugs, beautiful women, a limitless supply of money, fast cars, opulent homes, and the best liquors in the world; Conversely, many young women aspire to hook up with this type of guy, thinking her bad boy would protect her and live an everlasting life of luxury, like the Kardashians. Most times, however, the drug dealer will cheat on her with anything that breathes, beat her down physically or psychologically or both and make her feel like the scum of the earth to satisfy his ego. She may have money and the comforts that come with it, but she will never have peace. Television and movies often portray the life of a drug dealer in a glamorous way, but in reality, it is not all that it seems. Drug dealers do not trust anyone, not girlfriends or boyfriends, wives or husbands, brothers, sisters, cousins, or friends. In fact, the majority have no real friends.

A drug dealer is always worried about getting ripped off by the seller, the buyer, the distributor, or an independent cowboy who wants to rip people off, and this is not counting the Federal, State, or local police, all of whom are trying to nail them to the wall and take away the most valuable thing any human possesses, and that is freedom. They are a paranoid bunch, always looking over their respective shoulders for the police or maybe a rival, trying to take advantage of a lapse in judgment to assassinate him. Conversely, they are always trying to take advantage of less street-savvy individuals to make an easy score. They are manipulative and cunning, always planning their next score. Nevertheless, no matter how successful they are, how many millions or billions they have, or how untrusting they are, they are never untouchable.

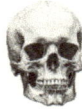

In 1978, at the age of fourteen, I landed my first job as a busboy at the renowned Fort Brown restaurant, a culinary gem in Brownsville, TX back then. The restaurant closed in the evenings, and the Resaca Club, an adjoining restaurant and nightclub, opened for business.

The Resaca club offered the finest dining available and featured some of the best nightclub acts south of San Antonio, Texas. Elegant dishes of prime rib, luscious steaks, succulent lobster, jumbo sized shrimp, crab, fish, and oysters freshly caught from the Gulf of Mexico were offered on the menu along with exquisite desserts, freshly prepared by the executive chef. The restaurant had an exclusive wine cellar with a variety of fine wines and spirits. The tables in the dining room were elegantly set and decorated, with cloth table covers and napkins shaped in exotic forms such as swans, peacocks, or roses, all of this melded with a picturesque window providing a breathtaking view of Brownsville's historic Horseshoe Lake. Customers came from all over the state to enjoy the show bands, dine and experience the highly entertaining, table side, flamed pepper steak and the flaming table side Bananas Foster for dessert. The restaurant was about five minutes from the Gateway International bridge that adjoined Brownsville, Texas to Matamoros, Mexico and it was a popular spot for many people in the valley, and also the Matamoros crime bosses. During my employment there, I caught a glimpse of the immense power that organized crime wielded.

I witnessed people being asked to leave their dinner tables to make room for the Matamoros crime bosses. Occasionally, I had to awkwardly inform a group of people that there was a reservation error, and they needed to switch tables. If the party resisted, which was often, the head waiter was called upon to explain the reason for the inconvenience, usually whispered into the ear of the leader of the group. They always complied and for their trouble, a complimentary bottle of wine or round of drinks was sent to their table. As a child, I was curious about why these things occurred, and when I asked about it, I was simply told to shut up, do as I was told, and go about my business—which I did. But the curiosity never left my mind. The way these people could move an entire family from their dinner table fascinated me. My father got me the job, because he was the Food and Beverage manager at the restaurant, and he wanted to keep me off the streets.

One weekend, I gathered the courage to ask my father to explain who these people were. I remember to this day, my father took a deep breath and told me, "Son, these people are like the mafia; just do as you are told; don't ask questions; don't upset them, make sure they are happy and collect your tip money at the end of the night and just go home." So, I did as I was told, unwittingly serving some of the biggest crime bosses in the area. I lit their cigarettes or cigars on command, refilling their wine or whiskey glasses, laughing with them as they made jokes at my expense, much like the Scorsese movie "Goodfellas" where the protagonists make fun of Spider, the waiter. I was probably the original Spider, in retrospect, except I didn't mouth off at them and didn't get killed. I did as I was told, but never forgot the power they wielded, and I believe this curiosity led me to my eventual career choice.

The jokes and ribbing were humiliating, but I was a good soldier and did my job with a smile. As most red-blooded, gullible four-teen-year-olds of modest means are, I was very impressionable. These guys spent an incredible amount of money, the majority of which was spent on booze, with actual food taking a slight backseat to the entire bill. They'd often leave the head waiter a tip as high as $500, of which I and my other partner made $20 each. For a fourteen-year-old kid in 1978, to make twenty bucks in one night was empowering. Of course, the majority would go to my mom for our family living expenses, but I still had some left over for movies, albums, magazines and other stupid things fourteen-year-old boys enjoyed.

I remember talking to my grandfather about these people, and how the power they projected intrigued me. His mood changed from peaceful to somber and stern when he told me that those people had what they had by doing bad things, and that one day they would either be in jail or dead. He told me that if I did the right thing, I would never have to fear anything; no matter how poor or rich you are, always do the right thing. My grandfather's prediction about these people's fate was soon proven right. One of the mob bosses that frequented the Resaca club was shot in an assassination attempt in Matamoros; the man survived and was taken to a Matamoros hospital, where within 24 hours, a team of hitmen entered the hospital to finish him off. They failed, however, and he survived. They whisked him out of the Matamoros hospital and transported him to Monterrey, Nuevo Leon, Mexico, where he eventually succumbed to his wounds. I realized right then and there that this was not the movies, a novella, or a corrido and you don't get to run off to some exotic island with a sexy girlfriend if you are involved in that business.

I remained captivated, despite the assassination attempt—or perhaps because of it. Their lifestyle mystified me. How did they get to be in that position? I didn't know at the time that my fascination would eventually lead me—30-years later—to be the leader of a team that would make their lives miserable and engage into in all-out war with them. Eventually, I would become a Special Agent with the DEA, and the DEA chose me to lead the DEA office in Monterrey as the Resident Agent in Charge. I didn't know what I didn't know.

My siblings enjoying the sunset on South Padre Island.

Chapter 2: History of DEA and its Role in Mexico

During my time with the DEA, I often found it surprising that many people were unaware of DEA's mission or the vast scope of its global operations. It maintains offices in over sixty-six countries within US Embassies or US Consulates worldwide. The DEA traces its roots back to the early 1900's, a time when cocaine was legal and used in the soft drink Coca-Cola, and when cough remedies contained heroin and opium. Just before the Pure Food and Drug Act was passed, Coca Cola removed cocaine from its beloved soft drink and replaced it with caffeine. The sale and distribution of heroin during that era had no oversight or control. After the Spanish American war, President Theodore Roosevelt convoked an international conference to control opium traffic, especially in the Far East, while doing nothing to combat the problem in the United States. The government enacted the Harrison Narcotics Act in 1914, which mandated the registration and taxation of individuals involved in the production and distribution of morphine, heroin, or coca products.

The law strictly prohibited individuals without medical credentials from obtaining a registration to sell, distribute, or manufacture narcotics. The Department of Treasury, Bureau of Internal Revenue enforced the narcotics laws under the Harrison Act, as it was classified as a tax law. When Prohibition was enacted in 1920, narcotics agents became part of the Prohibition unit within the Bureau of Internal Revenue, Treasury Department. Fifteen hundred agents were assigned to enforce the prohibition law. These agents were essentially battling against both narcotics smugglers and bootleggers, effectively fighting a two-front war. The birth of prohibition led to the closure of many breweries within the United States, allowing our border countries of Canada and Mexico to fill in the gap and keep up with the demand.

The prohibition era gave rise to professional Mexican smuggling groups, who were more than willing to supply the United States demand and capitalize on the huge profits made from the sale of alcohol on the black market. In South Texas specifically, Juan N. Guerra, who was the founder of what is now the Gulf Cartel and considered the Godfather of Cartel traffickers in Mexico and the US Border, started his empire by smuggling whiskey across the border from Matamoros to Texas and other cities in the Northern United States. Organized crime flourished during this era and also raked in huge profits on the black market with the establishment of speak easy lounges and private bars.

The agents found the work insurmountable, and in 1927, the pro-hibition unit separated from the Internal Revenue service. It became known as the Bureau of Prohibition, thus dividing responsibilities for Narcotic enforcement and Liquor enforcement between the two agencies. In 1930, President Herbert Hoover formed The Federal Bureau of Narcotics (FBN) and appointed Harry Ainslinger as the Commissioner of the newly established agency. During the 1930's, reports were being received of a marijuana use epidemic along the Mexican border as smugglers were now bringing marijuana along with liquor into the United States. The FBN, however, did not give marijuana investigations much priority as it would infringe on time spent on cocaine and heroin investigations, a mindset that still exists among certain regions of the country for DEA. In the 1950's, reports of Mexican opium surfaced in New York City, and individuals started refining the opium for distribution to other major cities in the United States. Also, The Herrera family based in Durango, Durango, Mexico were distributing multi hundred kilogram quantities of Mexican brown heroin into Chicago. In 1966, the Food and Drug Administration formed an enforcement arm called the Bureau of Drug Abuse Control (BDAC), whose responsibility was to control methamphetamine and hallucinogens. Their lifespan was short-lived as in 1968 the Johnson administration merged the FBN and BDAC into the Bureau of Narcotics and Dangerous Drugs (BNDD).

It should be noted that in 1963, the first offices of what is now DEA in Mexico opened in the United States Embassy in Mexico City and the United States Consulate in Monterrey, followed by offices in Guadalajara, Jalisco in 1969, Hermosillo in 1971, Mazatlán in 1973 and Merida in 1976, marking the beginning of their presence in the country. In 1973, President Nixon submitted a plan to Congress that would merge all Federal narcotics enforcement agencies to work to form one unit. The merging of the Bureau of Narcotics and Dangerous Drugs and the US Customs Service Drug Investigations Unit on July 1st, 1973 marked the birth of the US Drug Enforcement Administration—an agency that would forever change the landscape of drug enforcement in the United States.

In the early 1970's, my mentor and partner, Mario Alvarez, a BNDD agent, was stationed in Guadalajara. He shared stories with me about conducting undercover heroin buys on the bustling streets of Guadalajara alongside the Mexican Federal Judicial Police. Heroin that came directly from the Herrera family. During the 1970's, the cultivation and distribution of Mexican heroin increased because of intense law enforcement pressure on European heroin smugglers, in particular, the conspirators popularly known as the French Connection. The French connection involved the smuggling of raw opium from Turkey to Marseille, France, for refinement and eventual shipment into the United States through the Canadian Border. The French connection supplied as much as 90 percent of the heroin in the United States. Demand for Mexican heroin skyrocketed after the arrests of the French Connection conspirators and again, as they did during prohibition, Mexican traffickers were more than happy to meet the demand. By the mid-1970's, Mexican traffickers had gained control over three-quarters of the heroin market in the United States, thanks to the increasing presence of poppy fields in Durango, Guerrero, Sinaloa, Oaxaca, Chihuahua, Michoacan, and Jalisco. The United States experienced a rapid and concerning increase in heroin use during this time, largely because of the accessibility and affordability of Mexican heroin.

In 1974, astonishingly enough, the Government of Mexico requested technical assistance from the United States to eradicate poppy fields in the States of Sinaloa, and Guerrero but the effort was short-lived because of a lack of resources. In 1976, the United States and Mexico teamed up to form an opium eradication program targeting poppy fields throughout Mexico and spraying them with agent orange. The operation known as Operation Trizo was highly successful. Over 20,000 acres of poppy fields were destroyed in the operation—enough to produce eight tons of heroin. The operation led to the arrest of over four thousand people and caused a significant decrease in the purity of Mexican heroin. It was so successful that many villages in the poppy growing regions experienced an economic crisis. Because of the social unrest caused by the economic crisis, Mexico put an end to the eradication effort.

As the demand for heroin grew, so did the number of heroin investigations along the southwest border. US Agents, at the time, could cross the border into Mexico to expand their investigations and identify the heroin's source of supply. These cross border undercover operations came at great risk to the safety of DEA agents, as they had no Law Enforcement authority in Mexico. Usually when one thinks of DEA in Mexico, what immediately comes to mind is the tragic kidnap murder of Enrique "Kiki" Camarena, but there were other agents before Camarena who also suffered tragedies because of working in Mexico. For example, in June 1975, Special Agent Don Ware and his partner took part in one of these cross-border operations and attempted to make an undercover heroin purchase in San Luis Rio Colorado, Sonora. While they were on their way to make the buy, four individuals intercepted them and forced them to exit their vehicle. Then, the men searched them and found a gun on Ware's partner. They were then severely beaten and forced into the back of a pickup truck and driven into the vast Sonoran Desert, where they both believed they would be killed. Luckily, the men did not find Agent Ware's gun. The moment the truck stopped, Ware, in a heroic effort to escape death, opened fire, killing the driver instantly. A major shootout ensued with the other men, resulting in both Ware and his partner being hit twice by M-16 rounds. Ware survived despite being severely wounded. Ware would later recover and return to work for the DEA in a limited capacity but passed away in 2011 because of his wounds.

There is also the story of DEA pilots Ralph Shaw and James Lunn, who were both killed during a poppy eradication detail when their plane flew into a box canyon at low altitude. Pilot Lunn could not maneuver the airplane out of the canyon and the plane crashed north of Acapulco Guerrero in May 1976, during Operation Trizo.

In the mid to late 1980's, Colombian cocaine traffickers were losing loads in record quantities because of increased Law Enforcement pressure led by Vice President George Bush's South Florida Task Force. Maritime conveyances and private and commercial aircraft introduced around 80% of cocaine in the United States through South Florida. As more and more cocaine and money shipments were being lost to law enforcement efforts, Colombian traffickers were losing money and, obviously, that was not good for business. The Gulf Cartel was now being led by Juan N. Guerra's nephew, Juan Garcia-Abrego. The Gulf Cartel controlled the ports in the entire Gulf Coast region from the Yucatan Peninsula in Quintana Roo to the Texas-Mexico border in Matamoros Tamaulipas. The realm of the Gulf cartel also controlled the interior states of Nuevo Leon, Coahuila, San Luis Potosi and Zacatecas. Besides this territory, the Gulf Cartel controlled the border between Mexico and the United States from Matamoros, Tamaulipas to Piedras Negras, Coahuila, on the Mexican side of the border and Brownsville, Texas to Eagle Pass, TX, on the United States side of the border. This was the largest territory controlled by any single cartel in Mexico.

The Mexican traffickers had successfully smuggled contraband, including heroin and marijuana, into the United States since the days of prohibition, as mentioned earlier. Their smuggling routes and infrastructure were firmly established, leaving no room for error. An alliance between Colombian and Mexican drug trafficking organizations was a match made in heaven and both pounced on the opportunity. Eventually, multi ton quantities of Colombian cocaine were being shipped to Mexico via overland transport, aircraft or through maritime vessels for distribution in the United States; once sold, the multi-million dollar proceeds were shipped to Colombia minus the fee charged by the Mexican traffickers. It was a bonanza for both the Colombian and Mexican traffickers. The Colombians could not ship their cocaine fast enough to meet the demands. They even went to the extent of purchasing cargo jets and loading them with tons of cocaine for shipment to Mexico, where corrupt law enforcement officials protected the loads. The Gulf Cartel was not the only organization that took advantage of this newfound treasure trove; The Guadalajara Cartel, the Amado Carillo Fuentes organization, the Sinaloa cartel and the Arrellano-Felix organization were all thriving because of the shift in transport and distribution of cocaine through Mexico. Some estimate that over 330 tons of cocaine passed through Mexico and into the United States at this time, and this figure has significantly increased since the 1980's. Consequently, the role of DEA agents in Mexico grew increasingly vital for agents conducting investigations in the United States and Colombia.

Despite not receiving a formal education, Juan Garcia-Abrego showcased remarkable acumen and creativity as a businessman. He negotiated a deal with the Colombian organizations that would allow him to keep 50% of every cocaine load as payment for his distribution services. The math is simple. If the Colombian suppliers sent 1000 kilograms, which was basically the norm, Garcia kept 500 kilograms for himself. Not bad, considering the price per kilo in the mid-1980's hovered around $40 thousand dollars. That is a cool $20 million just off one load. This successful and profitable strategy allowed Garcia-Abrego, to rake in billions of dollars in proceeds annually. Multi-ton cocaine loads were flown into a ranch owned by Garcia-Abrego, in Soto La Marina, a sleepy fishing village south of Matamoros, Tamaulipas. Like a well-oiled machine, Gulf cartel members offloaded countless duffle bags stuffed with kilos of cocaine and transported them to Matamoros for eventual transport to stash houses in the Rio Grande Valley. From there, they broke down the loads into smaller shipments and transported them throughout the United States, including New York, Chicago, Los Angeles, and Miami. In October 1989, agents with the Texas Department of Public Safety seized 9 tons of Gulf Cartel cocaine in a stash house in Harlingen, Texas, valued at 3 billion dollars. In the same week, Coast Guard officials seized a vessel off the Yucatan Peninsula with 6 tons of Gulf Cartel cocaine valued at 2 billion dollars. These seizures are just a snapshot of the weight the Gulf cartel was moving at the time.

Garcia-Abrego was incredibly influential, earning comparisons to Pablo Escobar. He had politicians and law enforcement officials on his payroll, paying out several million dollars a month in bribes. Rumors also circulated that he had various US Law Enforcement officials on his payroll. Whatever the case, the FBI placed Garcia-Abrego on their ten most wanted list and Mexican Federal Judicial police, accompanied by DEA agents from the Monterrey Resident office, arrested him in Monterrey, Mexico in January 1996. They then extradited him to the United States in Houston, Texas on a DEA aircraft to face a multi-count indictment. After a four week trial, a jury convicted him of drug trafficking, money laundering, and operating a Continuing Criminal Enterprise. He was sentenced to eleven consecutive life terms. Garcia-Abrego's arrest set the stage for a fierce competition to fill the leadership void in the Gulf cartel, which was ultimately claimed by Osiel Cardenas Guillen.

Cardenas-Guillen garnered notoriety after he stopped a vehicle occupied by a DEA agent, FBI agent and source of information. The agents were surrounded by Osiel's gunmen, who attempted to kidnap all three and threatened to shoot them on the spot. Fortunately, they talked their way out of the situation and were eventually released unharmed. They were lucky, but neither DEA nor FBI ever forgot the incident.

It was during this shift in transport routes for cocaine in the mid-1980's that DEA started heavily recruiting Hispanic agents with bilingual abilities. Hispanic agents were in high demand for their ability to perform a range of tasks, including undercover work, defendant interviews, wiretap monitoring, conversation translation, and Spanish document analysis. I became one of the many recruits who joined DEA during this era, and I rose through the ranks as the years progressed and was promoted to the Supervisory level. My career path eventually led me to Mexico, where I was chosen to serve as the Resident Agent in Charge of the Monterrey Resident Office. I was fully aware of the inherent danger that came with this assignment.

The dangers of working in Mexico as a DEA agent have always been intrinsic to the position. Many people are unaware that DEA agents in Mexico cannot carry firearms and do not possess diplomatic immunity. Operating in one of the most dangerous and corrupt countries in the world, DEA agents face constant danger without any protection. If an agent just happens to be caught with a weapon or has to use it in some fashion, and manages to survive, he has no diplomatic protection, thus exposing him to prosecution by Mexican authorities and facing potential jail time. He is then swiftly exiled from the country, forever forbidden to set foot on its soil again.

Operating in those circumstances is tough, but we did, and we were good at it. We always found ways to make cases successful. It is part of working as a DEA agent in Mexico. But the job is not for everyone. One must be resilient, persistent, flexible, and possess extreme mental and emotional toughness. DEA agents do not get asked or forced to work in Mexico; we voluntarily apply for openings that interest us in the different offices in Mexico and compete with other agents for the privilege of working there. My colleagues who are still working down there in these challenging circumstances have my utmost respect.

Chapter 3: "El Puma"

I am often asked at family gatherings, restaurants and bars to tell a memorable story about my time as a DEA agent. There are many to tell throughout a night of jovial drinking but one stands out above all of them. But before I tell the story, I always ask the listeners and now I ask you, the reader; Do you believe in destiny or coincidence? Does a higher power predetermine our lives through destiny or are the events that occur in our lives circumstantial and random? I often ponder this question in solitude, whenever I am fishing the serene turquoise waters of the Laguna Madre, where time is of no importance, where seagulls and pelicans are my only companions. Was it destiny that once brought me face to face with the most feared drug lord, "El Puma", on the Southwest border? Or was it all a random set of circumstances throughout time that brought us face to face? Read the story and decide for yourself.

On February 2, 1987, I began my duty with the US Drug Enforcement Administration in my beloved hometown of Brownsville, TX. Following that, I endured sixteen grueling weeks of Basic Agent training in the frigid foothills of Quantico, Virginia at the DEA Academy, my first ever extended time away from home. Everything was new to me. The endless sea of Virginia pine, majestic maple and towering oak trees fascinated me, saturated in freshly fallen snow. I was fascinated by the significantly rich history of the region and most of all, I was fascinated with the diversity of classmates from all over the United States who shared the experience with me and who eventually became lifelong friends as members of Basic Agent class 48. During those sixteen weeks, the instructors put us through a rigorous physical training regime designed to thin out the herd and eliminate the weak, but nobody quit. We all took whatever they dished out and came back for more. The training was also designed to provide us with the mental strength necessary to react quickly and decisively when faced with adversity and critical situations, a skill that would serve to my advantage later in my career. The instructors taught us classes on law, evidence handling, interrogation techniques, surveillance, and undercover activities—anything that a DEA agent would have to do in the field—in the academy, or at least they attempted to. Because, in reality, no amount of training could ever prepare one for the real world.

We had the privilege of having the best of the best as instructors in our academy, but there was one instructor who stood out from the rest. Mr. C, a fellow Hispanic from Texas, instantly connected with me as soon as we met. He was a well-liked instructor, with an easy-going personality and was always approachable. I never once saw him berate a student or raise his voice to anyone, as most other instructors did occasionally. Mr. C had a fascinating story about his time in Mexico, and he dedicated three hours of class time one afternoon to share his story with us. Every single one of us in that room was awestruck. Mr. C had been in Guadalajara during the time of Enrique "Kike" Camarena's kidnapping. His role in the investigation had almost cost him his life, and he shared with us the steps he took mentally to survive his ordeal. It was one of the first times I had heard such a detailed account about the dangers one faced as a DEA agent in Mexico. His detailed account about life in Mexico as a DEA agent, the risks, and the dangers one faced, completely enthralled me. Although my career was in its early stages, I wanted to be a part of it. I knew, though, that one day I would have the opportunity to achieve my goal. I needed to take it one step at a time, and the first step meant graduating from the Academy.

In May 1987, my classmates and I graduated from the Academy as full-fledged Special Agents of the Drug Enforcement Administration. I was 22 years old, full of ambition, and ready to conquer the world. They assigned me to McAllen, TX, which is close to my hometown of Brownsville, Texas. At the time, Mexican Drug trafficking organizations had forged an alliance with Colombian cocaine suppliers who originally used South Florida as a staging point before distributing their loads to east coast cities in the United States. In 1982, Vice President George Bush formed the South Florida Task force to combat the enormous influx of cocaine coming into the region from Colombia. Although the Task Force was successful in seizing record amounts of cocaine, it really did not stop the flow of drugs coming into the country. It just educated the Colombians into expanding their distribution routes and they cast their eyes squarely on Mexico. It was the perfect fit. Mexican contraband smugglers already had reliable and well-established smuggling routes on the entire Southwest United States border that had been in their families for generations. An affiliation with the Colombian suppliers would be extremely lucrative for both sides. Both sides benefited from the situation, and as a result, large quantities of cocaine began entering the Southwest Border, including the Rio Grande Valley and my new assignment in McAllen, TX.

In 1984, as the head of the Gulf Cartel, Juan Garcia Abrego reigned as the king of cocaine in Mexico and the Rio Grande valley The institutional knowledge Abrego gained through his uncle Juan N Guerra, a longtime notorious bootlegger and smuggler from Matamoros, Mexico proved invaluable when the Colombians came calling. The Gulf Cartel oversees possibly the largest swath of territory on the Southwest border, ranging from Matamoros all the way to Piedras Negras, Mexico and all ports of entries in between. The Gulf Cartel was raking in the money because of the Colombian alliance, with estimates of gross revenue at about 2 billion a year. An empire such as this required many trusted underlings in various roles in several parts of the country to oversee off loading or loading of cocaine deliveries; counting, delivering and laundering cash proceeds, protecting stash houses, recruiting and hiring of pilots to transport large cocaine loads from Colombia to Mexico, recruiting and hiring of ranch hands to take care of livestock and maintain the upkeep of the various ranches owned by Abrego, and delivering bribe payments to government officials and Law Enforcement. So, Garcia assigned proven and trusted members of Abrego's circle, known as Plaza Bosses, in key cities throughout Tamaulipas to oversee these critical activities for the continuity of the organization.

In the early to mid-1990's, the Gulf Cartel arguably had every Municipal and Tamaulipas Law Enforcement official on their vast payroll. One of these state Policemen was a homicide detective in Reynosa, Tamaulipas, Carlos Landin Martinez. His peers and superiors considered Landin an exceptional cop, but unfortunately, being a good cop in Mexico doesn't pay the bills or put food on the table. What it does is catch the eyes of the leadership of the Gulf cartel. Gregorio Sauceda-Gamboa, aka "El Goyo", recruited Landin into the shadow of the Gulf Cartel, where he became one of several hundreds of cops who served as the eyes and ears in the State of Tamaulipas for Goyo and the Gulf cartel.

Landin proved his worth to the Gulf Cartel and quickly moved up in the hierarchy of the Reynosa Plaza. Using his position as a state policeman, Landin brazenly recovered marijuana, and cocaine loads that the Federal and State Police had seized from their respective evidence vaults and returned the loads to the Gulf Cartel, earning him honors and accolades among the Gulf cartel leadership. After Abrego's arrest in 1996, a power struggle emerged for leadership of the Gulf Cartel, and eventually, Osiel Cardenas Guillen took control. Osiel Cardenas Guillen was a cold, calculating killer who took no prisoners and earned the nickname "El Mata Amigos" (Friend Killer). El Goyo remained as the Reynosa Plaza Boss after Guillen took the leadership role, and as a result Landin moved up in the ranks of the cartel, as Goyo's second in command and Chief enforcer for Reynosa.

Landin's good fortune extended to his role in the Tamaulipas state police. No longer was he a mere homicide detective, but the commander of the State homicide unit in Reynosa. As part of his cartel duties, Landin ensured that any organization moving drug loads through the Reynosa Plaza paid the required tributary fee to the Gulf cartel or else he ensured they paid the price in the most violent manner, and in effect, made an example out of them so other traffickers would not try the same tactic. He oversaw the transportation of large amounts of cocaine and marijuana from Mexico into the United States via the Rio Grande River for temporary storage in the Rio Grande valley and eventual distribution to various parts of the Northern United States. He also oversaw the transportation of the proceeds derived from the sale of these cocaine and marijuana loads back to Mexico for eventual laundering. The proceeds amounted to several million dollars on a weekly basis, of which he took a percentage for his role as second in command. Violence was part of the job, and he performed well, having received plenty of practice as a member of the State Police. Any cartel member who was dumb enough to lose a cartel load, soon would have the distinct pleasure of a face-to-face meeting with Landin. If the answers to his questions were not to his satisfaction, that person unfortunately learned the exact magnitude of Landin's penchant for violence.

In 1999, he was dismissed from his duties as Commander of the State Police homicide unit, but he remained unfazed by the loss. The money he was making as a member of the Gulf Cartel was beyond anything he could have imagined, dwarfing the earnings he would have had as a State Police commander. His role in the Cartel took on an even more significant role as the acting Plaza Boss, because his boss, "El Goyo," fell deeply into the dark and hellish abyss of cocaine and alcohol addiction. El Goyo's condition had deteriorated to where he couldn't make important decisions, so Landin stepped in and essentially took on the role of the Plaza Boss for Reynosa. Life was good for Landin, and he flourished in the powerful role as Chief Enforcer and acting Plaza Boss, earning the respect of other cartel leaders, including the new boss Osiel Cardenas Guillen.

In a peculiar twist, my career path and Landin's seemed to run parallel to each other. In 1998, I earned the position of back-up Group Supervisor for my assigned Enforcement Group, just like Landin's promotion within the ranks of the Gulf cartel and State Police. I had no clue who Carlos Landin was, nor did I know of his existence, and I am most sure that he had not the slightest idea of mine. In the fall of 2000, DEA selected me for my first foreign assignment in Guadalajara, Jalisco, Mexico, also known as the Pearl of the Pacific. Guadalajara is the second largest city in Mexico, the cradle of the ruthless Guadalajara cartel, and the city in which the most infamous crime against a United States federal agent occurred: the Enrique Camarena, kidnap, torture, and murder carried out by the Guadalajara Cartel. The first time I flew into Guadalajara, I was awestruck. I could not fathom that I was flying into the same airport where the Arellano-Felix brothers tried to assassinate Chapo Guzman but killed Roman Catholic Cardinal Juan José Posadas Ocampo instead, unleashing chaos within both organizations.

Despite the passage of 15 years since Kike's murder, the tension remained palpable whenever we met with our Mexican counterparts. Despite the pervasive sense of mistrust and resentment, we knew that interacting with them was necessary to effectively fulfill our job. We were after all guests in their country, and we had no arrest powers. Sometimes, we were stonewalled, other times we were treated like royalty. I guess it depended on what kind of mood the person we were dealing with had awoken to. We were a small office, as most offices in Mexico are, comprising four agents: one intelligence analyst, the Resident Agent in Charge and two administrative assistants. Many times, during my tour in Guadalajara, I recalled the advice of my mentor and partner, Mario Alvarez. Sheltered in the darkness of the Toucan cantina, from the blistering heat of the South Texas sun and cooled by free-flowing pitchers of frosty cold beers, he told me: "Don't get lost in all the work. There will be plenty of it. Enjoy your time over there. Absorb the culture. Get to know the city and its beauty, make friends away from the office, take the family to see the sights. There are many places to go and much to do over there. Enjoy yourself and make it memorable for your family as well."

I never forgot his words, and I took them to heart. Our lives were filled with excitement as we pursued some of the biggest traffickers on the planet, such as Armando Valencia, Sandra Ávila Beltrán, Ramon and Benjamin Arellano-Felix, Ignacio "Nacho" Colonel, Juan Jose Esparragoza-Moreno aka "El Azul", Ismael "Mayo" Zambada, and Joaquin "El Chapo" Guzman, a distinguished list of members in the drug trafficking world. But we were also privileged to experience the finest that the Mexican culture offered. For starters, aside from my fascination with the history of narcotics traffickers that permeated the city, Guadalajara emits a mysterious beauty, rich history, culture, and culinary perfection. The picturesque vision of the streets of Guadalajara lined with Jacaranda trees blooming robustly, with an endless variety of purple hues, is nothing short of enchanting—a vision that will eternally remain engraved in the recesses of my mind.

Established in 1542, Guadalajara also known as the Pearl of the Pacific and the city of roses, is the capital of Jalisco, the birthplace of mariachi music, tequila and the home to many famous authors, actors, artisans, and musicians, including the iconic and legendary Vicente Fernandez. It is the second largest city in Mexico with a population of approximately 8 million residents. Despite frequent destruction by fires and many earthquakes, the Cathedral de Guadalajara remains one of the oldest cathedrals in Mexico. The cathedral's history is fascinating and filled with dark irony. The cathedral houses the body of Cardinal Juan Jesus Posadas Ocampo, who assassins killed at the Guadalajara airport in 1993 because of the Arellano Felix and Chapo Guzman conflict. It serves as an eternal testament to the rampant violence unleashed by the cartels, dragging innocent citizens into its deadly wake.

It is difficult not to fall in love with the city, with its rich architecture, both colonial and modern. Art abounds in the city and surrounding areas. The cities of Tonala and Tlaquepaque are homes to some of the finest artisans in the country and thousands of tourists and locals alike make weekend trips to the cities to purchase artwork, artisan furniture, colorful folkloric costumes or maybe just to try some of the local tortas ahogadas, (drowned subway). The torta gets its name "drowned" because the sandwich is soaked in a red chili sauce made from fresh chile de arbol, and it typically contains a generous portion of succulent golden fried pork meat marinated in lime, garlic, and red onions. I recommend you have a cold beverage readily available to counteract the incoming heat that awaits your palate. Local lore explains that this dish, native to Guadalajara, came to fruition by accident. According to legend, a local customer ordered a torta and specifically asked for it to be topped off with the spicy salsa mix. Allegedly, the vendor accidentally dropped the entire torta into the sauce bowl, drowning it completely, thus giving birth to the now famous Torta Ahogada de Jalisco. Many nights after endless rounds of tequilas, beer and mariachis, my friends and I have indulged in these famously spicy pork sandwiches to calm the effects of the ensuing painful hangover that threatened to debilitate our productivity the next day. In my two years in Guadalajara, I tried exploring as much as I could about this fascinating city because there is so much to see and immerse oneself in. One thing I can say is that its beauty is captivating, the people down to earth and friendly, the music unforgettable and iconic and of course, I need not say anything about the work, nor the evil and sinister dark side that lurks in every corner of this beautiful city. Regretfully, that side speaks for itself.

The Guadalajara Resident office had a large-scale area of responsibility, which covered six states: Jalisco, Nayarit, Colima, Guanajuato, Aguascalientes, and Zacatecas. Our job involved building relationships with law enforcement officials, cultivating reliable sources of information, and gathering intelligence on drug-related activities in each of those regions. Each of those states had their own police entities at the Federal, State, and municipal level and we were expected to have contacts in each of those states. We had our hands full with just the city of Guadalajara, the second largest city in Mexico, with a population of 8 million people. An insurmountable task for only four agents. As a comparison, in the United States, DEA offices had Enforcement Groups composed of numerous agents, sometimes up to twelve or fourteen agents, to carry out their responsibilities in their assigned areas. We were only four. As typical law enforcement officers do worldwide, we made light of a difficult situation and joked that each one of us was the equivalent to an Enforcement Group in the states and we made the best of the situation. The way we saw it, there was no way to develop relationships with our Mexican counterparts unless we personally met with and interacted with them. That meant we had to travel to every state within our area of responsibility. I was more than happy to do my part.

I made my first trip as an agent in Guadalajara to the famous tourist destination Puerto Vallarta, Jalisco to meet the commander of the Federal police in that city. Although the city is a world-renowned tourist destination, there is a dark underbelly that thrives in Vallarta. Vallarta was the playground for Rafael Caro Quintero, Ernesto Fonseca Carrillo and various other members of the Guadalajara Cartel including Ignacio Colonel, a major cocaine trafficker bringing 20-ton quantities of cocaine into Vallarta via maritime shipments from Colombia. The Arellano Felix brothers also frequented Vallarta to party and conduct negotiations with other notorious traffickers for large cocaine shipments. In 1992, Chapo Guzman sent a hit team to kill Benjamin and Ramon Arellano's team while they were celebrating Benjamin's birthday at the Christine Disco, resulting in the deaths of six people. It was in fact a narco playground and one didn't really know who one was going to run into at any given time in Vallarta. The vibe the city gave off was thrilling, upbeat, and festive, with the edge of danger mixed into the recipe. One always had the ominous sense that shit could hit the fan anywhere, anytime, at any minute or any second.

To get to Vallarta, one can take a quick one-hour flight from Guadalajara, take a long, miserable and harrowing bus trip through the Sierra Madre Occidental Mountain range, or one can drive out there. Our budget did not allow for a flight, and I certainly would not take a bus trip, so my partner and I took the five-hour scenic drive through what is arguably the most beautiful countryside in all of Mexico. It's hard not to marvel at the endless sea of blue agaves that engulf the countryside, merging perfectly with the Sierra Madre mountains and the golden sunlight peeking through the misty clouds drifting lazily over the sleepy town of Tequila, Jalisco. the birthplace of the national libation of Mexico, Tequila. The endless sea of agaves gave way to lush tropical foliage of mango, coconut, banana, and papaya trees flourishing in the fertile volcanic grounds of the Sierra Madre Mountains as swarms of colorful parrots descended upon the immense emerald, green jungle of fruit trees to roost before sundown. As we passed through the mountain region, the first glimpse of the Pacific coastline of Jalisco did not disappoint as the sun seemed to evaporate into the vast deep blueness of the Pacific, painting a bedazzling watercolor canvas of pink, purple, gray and burnt orange across the western sky, as dusk slowly fell over the city of Puerto Vallarta.

It was almost impossible to believe that in this small corner of celestial paradise, danger lurked around every corner. We met the commander for breakfast at a quaint restaurant on the Marina, far away from the tourist area and hidden among the many other shops and restaurants in the area. He was a well-built young man, sporting a military haircut, dark Ray Ban Aviator sunglasses, with blue jeans, a white crewneck shirt covered by a sharp blue blazer. He was armed, and three rough-looking bodyguards, who were also part of the Federal police, accompanied him. After exchanging pleasantries, he took off his sunglasses, ordered coffee and enthusiastically recommended the shrimp omelet, which we quickly agreed to order.

"No se van a arrepentir. Este desayuno es como probar parte del Cielo," he said, which means you will not regret it. This dish is like tasting a piece of paradise.

We also ordered coffee, trying to clear our heads from the effects of too much tequila and beer from the night before. We sat quietly, waiting for our food.

In Mexico, it is impolite to start off a business meeting talking business right off the bat, so we politely asked him the requisite background questions and found out that he was originally from Sinaloa and had joined the Federal Police after a brief stint in the Mexican Army. He had only been in his new assignment as commander for two weeks. His eyes glanced around shiftily, looking for any sign of danger that may lie in wait, as his bodyguards did the same. Our food arrived, and we eagerly delved into culinary perfection. The omelet comprised of freshly caught jumbo shrimp chopped into small, delightful morsels, folded into the omelet along with bell pepper, green onion, and Monterey jack cheese. The chef garnished the plate with parsley and accompanied it with a side of fresh avocado slices topped with sour cream. Each forkful seemed to dissolve slowly into your palate and on your taste buds. It was indeed heaven.

Interrupting our spellbound culinary bliss, the commander cleared his throat, took a gulp of coffee, and spoke softly, "Puede ser que no dure en Vallarta mucho tiempo," (there is a good chance that I will not be in Vallarta for much longer.)

My partner and I exchanged curious glances, and I blurted out, "Pero como? Si acaba de llegar aqui!" (But how? You just got here.)

We listened intently as we wolfed down our shrimp omelets. He explained that three days after his arrival, he received a disturbing message from some scary people, namely Benjamin and Ramon

Arellano-Felix. The message came as a fancy and expensive Don Julio
tequila bottle, wrapped with a big, bright red bow. Attached to the
bottle was a small red envelope with a handwritten message: Bien-
venido, a Vallarta comandante. Pronto nos veremos. Attentamente
Benjamin y Ramon Arellano Felix. The note translated to: Welcome
to Vallarta commander. We shall see each other soon. Cordially Benjamin and Ramon Arellano-Felix.

In a slow and almost whispered tone, he informed us he accepted
the position in Vallarta solely because nobody else desired it, and
his superiors compelled him to take it. He said he thought he was
chosen because he was young and from Sinaloa, making him an easy
target for control by the major trafficking organizations in the area,
such as the Arellano-Felix brothers, who were currently at war with
Joaquin Chapo Guzman. Glancing towards his bodyguards, who sat
at a table near the entrance of the restaurant, his fear was palpable. He
told us that the security detail was assigned to him by his superiors,
and he was sure that they were reporting the details of his day-to-day
activities to them and to the traffickers. He had told them he would
be meeting members of the US Consulate and had not mentioned
that we were DEA agents. Suddenly, what was probably the most
delicious omelet that I had ever tasted in my life became stuck in my
throat. A foreboding sense of anxiety and fear momentarily overcame
me as I tried to process his unsettling words. It took all the skill
and experience of undercover work that I learned over the previous
fourteen years to help us get through the meeting without giving up
our identities as agents. We told jokes, talked about sports, talked
about the beautiful women that abounded in Jalisco, talked about
horseracing, anything but the topic of drug trafficking, just to get
us to the end of the meeting and get the hell out of there. That was

my introduction to working in Mexico and Jalisco, the Pearl of the Pacific, the City of Roses.

I took my old partner's advice and made the best out of my time in Guadalajara. One of our areas of responsibilities was Manzanillo Colima, a major port city in Mexico and a favorite port destination for staggering amounts of cocaine coming into the port on container ships from Colombia, Ecuador, Peru, and other countries. Trust me, there is no better way to wait for a container ship to come into port than to wait at El Bigotes, an open-air restaurant bar on the shoreline of the Manzanillo beach enjoying an ice-cold Pacifica beer as the waves rumble, crash, and roar leaving a swirling foamy trail upon the golden sands. We almost felt a little guilty for indulging ourselves as we waited for our container ship, but the feeling didn't last too long. Especially when the server brought out our orders of mouthwatering "Pina tropical," a large serving of shrimp, fish and octopus ceviche mixed with chunks of fresh avocado, pineapple and mango, with a scattering of jalapeno morsels, all stuffed within a carved out, halved pineapple. The piquancy of the jalapenos fused perfectly with the sweet succulence of the pineapple and mango chunks, driving one's taste buds into a frenzy of flavor, almost obliging one to take a long swill of frosty cold beer before the next savory mouthful. Work did not have to be dreadful at all. We did not seize any cocaine on our container ship that day. Sometimes you win and more often than not, you don't. But we sure had a hell of a time and came back for work frequently, never failing to make our traditional pit stop at El Bigotes.

In Morelia Michoacan, I had the wonderful opportunity to immerse myself in the enchanting colonial architecture of the historic center. The Catedral de Morelia, with its intricate details and imposing presence, left me in awe. The Plaza de Armas, bustling with locals and visitors, provided a vibrant atmosphere. And discovering the birthplace of Jose Maria Morelos, La Casa Natal de Morelos, was a poignant reminder of the city's role in shaping Mexican history. Comparable to Jalisco's agave vast acreage of agave fields are the endless orchards of avocado fields that make Michoacan the largest importer of avocados to the United States in the world. Unfortunately, during my time there, two rival cartels engaged in a fierce war for control of the port of Lazaro Cardenas, making the city a dangerous place to stay for an extended visit. My partner and I also traveled to the city of Aguascalientes to assist Federal prosecutors in the seizure of 2 tons of cocaine from a Lear jet sent directly from Colombia. During this trip, we met Mexico's Attorney General, Rafael Macedo de la Concha, who oversaw the Mexican Army dousing the cocaine load with jet fuel and setting it ablaze in a magnificent display of fire. No exaggeration. After all the work was over, we partook in a bottle of wickedly delicious red wine produced from one of the local vineyards and paired it with a New York strip marinated in cognac and topped with mushrooms, wine sauce, a hefty serving of guacamole, with sour cream on the side—the best steak I have ever had.

After traveling throughout much of Mexico and enjoying its unique beauty, such as visiting the pyramids in Mexico City or witnessing smoke billowing into the sky from the bowels of the Popocatepetl volcano with a crimson sunrise as the backdrop, I received a promotion to Supervisory Special Agent and returned to McAllen, TX.

I still had no clue about El Puma's existence.

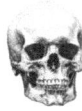

In McAllen, I took on the responsibility of overseeing the High Intensity Drug Task Force. This task force comprised of six DEA special agents and a multitude of state and local task force agents from nearby police departments and the Texas Department of Public Safety. I felt as though someone had handed me the keys to a brand-new Ferrari, and I couldn't wait to test drive it. Every single member of that group champing at the bit to make a big seizure or open a big case. Not long after I arrived in McAllen, my boss called me into his office and told me that an anonymous tip had come in regarding an individual that went by the nickname "El Comandante." He was a member of the Gulf Cartel, and he managed the logistics and transportation of large amounts of cocaine into the US before temporarily storing it in the McAllen area prior to transportation to northern US cities. "El Comandante" was also in charge of transporting the proceeds derived from the sale of cocaine loads back to Mexico. The only lead we had to identify "El Comandante" was a Mexican phone number from Reynosa, Tamaulipas, Mexico. My boss told me to run with the info and expand it into a viable case. Although I felt as though my abilities as an agent/investigator were being tested, I was not afraid to meet the challenge.

I assigned the case to one of the most fervent DEA agents in the group, Jimmy Bird. Jimmy was a GS-12 and was urgently seeking a promotion to the highly coveted GS-13 spot. Becoming a GS-13 not only meant a significant bump in pay, but it also meant one can apply for choice openings in both foreign and domestic offices.

Jimmy wanted desperately to relocate to his hometown of Houston, Texas. So, I assigned the lead to Jimmy and really thought little of it.

I knew that most traffickers use burner phones that are difficult to track down, especially in Mexico. If we were lucky, the phone service would be Telcel, a national company that we could get records from. However, most traffickers were using Nextel radio phones to communicate back and forth from the US and Mexico. But as my partner Mario Alvarez used to say, it is better to be lucky than good. I had confidence in Jimmy and if there was anything there, he would find it.

As it turned out luck was, indeed, on our side this time as Telcel, the largest cell phone service provider in Mexico, serviced the phone. The problem is that US agents from McAllen, Texas, could not get the records. We would need help from our agents in Monterrey, Mexico, to persuade their vetted team to help us get the records from Telcel. I did it regularly as an agent in Guadalajara, so it was not really a big deal. Having worked with agents stationed in Monterrey, I sent an e-mail to the Resident Agent in Charge (RAC), a friend of mine. Calling him was not an option as it was common knowledge that phones from the US Consulate were not secure enough to discuss sensitive information. So, I sent an e-mail to him, and he agreed to assign an agent to assist Jimmy in obtaining records for the phone and anything else that we may need to help us identify the holder of the phone.

Conducting a complex investigation requires tons of patience and lots of time-consuming and mundane work such as analyzing phone records. Television shows never depict this type of inane grunt work. The star detective on TV has phone records, analysts and high-tech equipment at his disposal producing immediate results. The reality is that a highly detailed analysis takes time. However, my boss kept asking me about the status of the case and I pestered Jimmy about it. After several weeks, he provided both me and my boss with the results of his work. Our Mexican counterparts in Monterrey had provided Jimmy with a call frequency report and from that report Jimmy identified two numbers in McAllen that were called several hundred times in a one-month time span. Jimmy identified Ricardo Muniz and Cantalicia Garza, Ricardo's ex-wife, as the holders of those phones. A detailed analysis of their phones opened our eyes to an intricate network of players working within the organization. Jimmy learned that Muniz and Garza called the Mexican number daily, among other numbers in Dallas, Houston, and Atlanta, Georgia. The case had the potential to identify the international source of supply, logistics coordinators, transportation specialists, buyers, distributors all the way down to street level distributors. Through interviews with cooperators, Jimmy learned that Cantalicia was originally from Reynosa, Tamaulipas and had two brothers, Juan Oscar Garza and Josue Garza. The icing on the cake from all the information Jimmy had gathered was the identification of the holder of the phone, Juan Oscar Garza alias "El Comandante," alias "El Barbas," a key leadership figure within the Gulf Cartel. We sat in stunned silence after Jimmy finished his briefing. The wheels were turning in our collective minds in developing an effective strategy to attack the organization and dismantle its infrastructure, a daunting task that would require close coordination with offices throughout the United States and Mexico. My boss finally broke the silence and said, "The first thing we are going to need is resources, so we must submit a proposal to the Organized Crime Drug Enforcement Task Force and request funding, manpower and a federal prosecutor assigned to the case. This is great work, Bird, but it is only the beginning. Start working on the proposal ASAP. Silva, in the meantime I want you to write up a detailed summary on this case so we can send it up to all the different offices that may have players in their regions and to our folks in Washington DC Headquarters, Mexico City and Monterrey, so we can get them on board with support as well. I want this summary within five business days. Let's get to work on this ASAP!" On that note, he got up and left the room. Jimmy could hardly contain his excitement.

"Great job Jimmy. This is your time to shine, my man! This is your chance to get your thirteen. Let's go get 'em!"

We shook hands and went to work on one of the biggest and most exciting cases in our lives.

I wrote up the summary in three days because it was important that the brass in headquarters recognize the significance of this case. Usually, headquarters only focused their resources on Field Divisions in major cities such as New York, Chicago, Miami, and Los Angeles. It would take an extraordinary case for the brass to focus on a Podunk city on the border, such as McAllen, Texas. Hell, I bet ninety-five percent of the folks in Headquarters didn't even know where McAllen was on the map, even though the Texas border is the primary transit points for large amounts of cocaine, marijuana, heroin, and crystal meth brought into the United States that eventually make their way to cities such as New York, Chicago, Miami and Los Angeles. Also, the millions and millions of dollars generated by the sale of those drugs in those large Field Divisions eventually came back to the US border, even through the Podunk town of McAllen, Texas. I was aware of this headquarters mentality, and I wanted to make sure that they knew exactly how McAllen played a significant role in the workings of narcotics distribution and money laundering throughout the country. Once the summary went out to headquarters and all the other offices involved, everyone knew exactly where McAllen was located and the potential this case carried. Now we had their attention.

The case became designated as a priority case and an official Organized Crime Drug Enforcement Task Force (OCDETF) investigation, which got us additional funding and a US Attorney assigned to the case. Everything was in place, now we just had to work the case.

There is an adage within the Law enforcement community that says "It is not what you know, it is what you can prove that is important." In our case, we knew that Ricardo Muniz was the logistics operator in the McAllen area for the Gulf Cartel and we knew he was making extensive use of his cell phone to coordinate the delivery of cocaine and marijuana loads to northern Texas and US cities and then arranging the pickup and delivery of millions of dollars in US currency for delivery to Mexico. But we had to prove it, and clearly state what evidence we had and articulate these facts on an affidavit for a federal judge to approve and authorize the intercept. So, we set in motion a strategy that had never been attempted before in the history of DEA. Our strategy was to have our Mexican counterparts, in conjunction with our office in Monterrey, to intercept Juan Oscar Garza's phone and listen to a narcotics related call—what we term a "dirty call"—then use that specific conversation as our probable cause in our affidavit for Muniz's phone. Sounds easy, right? I learned throughout my law enforcement career that absolutely nothing is easy. In order for us to legally use evidence off a Mexican wiretap, that wiretap must be a judicial wiretap, a wiretap that has been approved by a federal judge in Mexico. In order to get a judicial wiretap, our counterparts also had to prove that Juan Oscar was using his cellphone to conduct narcotics related activity. Proof that neither they nor we had.

Back to square one.

I have to give credit where credit is due. Although it was time consuming, our counterparts worked their asses off and came through with the evidence to get the judicial wiretap and start listening to Garza's activities. It was a wealth of information, and within a few weeks we had Muniz and Garza on an extensive call discussing the delivery of a load of cocaine in the United States. Exactly the kind of call we needed for our US affidavit for Muniz's phone. Once we could listen in on Muniz's phone, the floodgates broke open. Just as we had anticipated, Muniz's phone activity helped us identify drivers, some of whom had been arrested and had called Muniz for help with family expenses. These arrested drivers would later be located and interviewed regarding their ties to Muniz and for further intelligence on the organization. We seized cocaine loads, marijuana loads, and significant amounts of money. Throughout 2006, we spent a significant amount of time listening to Muniz, his wife Cantalicia Garza, and Juan Oscar discussing load deliveries, arguing about money, and Muniz's paranoid fears of being followed. He was not wrong about that, because we followed Muniz almost 24/7 for months. The best part was that they didn't have a clue where the leak in their organization came from. They had no idea that they, themselves were digging their own grave every time they picked up the phone to talk dope. We seized so much cocaine, marijuana and money that the higher-ranking members of the Gulf Cartel and Zetas suspected Carlos Landin and Garza. Despite these suspicions, Garza never stopped using the phone.

Cantalicia "Canti" Garza was always considered the financial brain of the organization. She used profits from narcotics loads to purchase properties in and around Reynosa to give the appearance of legitimacy. One of these properties was a nightclub called Club 57, in which they invested hundreds of thousands of dollars in renovations to make it one of the finest night clubs in Reynosa and to inaugurate the club they had hired Gloria Trevi, one of the most prolific singers of the time, to perform at the grand opening. One could feel the excitement and the energy in Canti's voice as she made last-minute preparations for the Grand opening. Juan Oscar felt a certain apprehension about attending the grand opening and he let Canti know about his gut feeling. They both agreed not to attend the grand opening but would instead go to the sound check the day before the grand opening to meet Trevi in person. Unfortunately for them, our counterparts from AFI heard the entire conversation. It was a perfect time for an enforcement operation. Juan Oscar, Canti and their other brother Omar all attended the sound check. They could knock off three birds in one fell swoop.

On April 17, 2007, AFI and SEDENA (Mexican Army), after receiving confirmation that the Garzas were all at Club 57, stormed the place and immediately arrested them. The arrest created shock waves throughout the entire Gulf Cartel and Zeta leadership, especially Carlos Landin Martinez, who was already under suspicion by the organization for losing narcotics and large amounts of money. At some point after the arrests of the Garzas, Landin Martinez decided he was no longer safe in Reynosa and crossed the Rio Grande River into the United States, setting up shop somewhere in McAllen, TX. It would be one of several decisions Landin would regret.

Despite receiving information from multiple sources, we had no clue about Landin's whereabouts after the Garza's arrests as the phone activity abruptly ceased. We conducted numerous aerial surveillances of known Gulf cartel hangouts for days on end but had no luck. We put the word out to our informants that if they heard anything, no matter how insignificant it may seem, to let us know immediately and they would be handsomely rewarded. But there was nothing. No leads. No new information.

In May 2007, Jimmy Bird testified before a Federal Grand jury and laid out the evidence against each member of the organization that we had identified in the conspiracy. However, we did not want to pull the trigger on arresting them because we were afraid Landin would get spooked if he really were in town and we suddenly arrested Muniz and everyone else. So, we waited patiently.

It was a scorching hot day on July 14, 2007, not unlike most summer days in deep south Texas. The kids were out of school and were eager to take a dip in the pool. I decided I would barbecue some burgers for the kids, and some ribs for some friends and family who would visit later in the afternoon. Because of all the pressure we had been under during the investigation, I had not celebrated my birthday. But today I was going to forget about work and celebrate my birthday the way any self-respecting Texan would celebrate, with beer and barbecue, surrounded by friends and family. I had the ribs marinating in my special marinade of pineapple juice, lime juice, soy sauce and a tinge of ginger and I had just lit the charcoal in my old pit when my wife came out to tell me she was going to make a quick run to the store because I had forgotten to buy her favorite side dish, corn, when I bought the meat earlier. I'm not sure what compelled me to assure her it was alright and that I would fetch the corn, while she stayed at home and supervised the kids in the pool. I have often thought about that specific moment and wonder what would have happened if I had not gone.

I took my wife's gray 2002 Ford Focus with a "Hello Kitty" sticker in the rear windshield and hauled ass to the grocery store. The layout of the store was as familiar to me as the back of my hand. I knew it so well I could probably run through the entire store blindfolded and still find whatever I needed. I got my shopping cart, went straight to the produce section, and parked my shopping cart in front of the corn section. Carefully shucking the hulls and inspecting each ear, I started in on the corn to make sure there were no defects on the kernels, intent on getting home to cook the ribs and burgers.

As I was inspecting one ear of corn, three men turned the corner from the meat section into the produce section. I locked eyes briefly with a stocky built older man with grayish hair. The two men with him were much younger and walked behind the older man, in deference to his authority. They all passed by me on my right-hand side. I noticed that one of the younger men put his hand on the older man's back, in a somewhat protective posture. I had seen the old man somewhere. The old computer in my brain started a file search in the most cavernous, obscure, and remote depths of my intellect. It transported me back to my office, to my desk, where I had posted a picture of Carlos Landin Martinez on the wall next to my door. Every day, for two years, the picture stared at me callously, devoid of feeling, almost mockingly.

I immediately went into high gear. Before taking any further action, I had to confirm for a fact that it was Landin, without a doubt. I watched them as they made their way in the produce section to the watermelon section. Landin himself picked out a large watermelon and gave it to one of the younger guys to inspect. I pushed my shopping cart closer to them so I could get a better look and confirm that it was Landin. I passed within 8 feet of him and got a good look at his face and confirmed that it was him. He glanced up as I passed them by, and we locked eyes again. The adrenalin was surging through every artery in my body, pumping out charges of electricity through my bloodstream. I could feel my carotid artery pulsating as the adrenaline flooded my blood stream. They placed their watermelon into their shopping cart and went to the checkout. While I was standing in line about four aisles away, I watched them through my peripheral vision, careful not to spook them or lose sight of them. I went through the checkout and paid for the corn, trying to fit in with the rest of the customers, despite wearing a shirt with the official DEA logo over the left side of my chest. I would not get close enough for him to notice that minor detail. They finished paying for the watermelon and they walked out of the north side exit of the store. I had parked on the south side, which could pose a problem for me, and I prayed they had not parked on the north side of the store—if they had, I might not get to see their vehicle.

Luckily, they were relaxed, taking their time to walk through the parking lot. I got the bag of corn, ran to the south side of the store, and quickly got into my wife's "Hello Kitty" car just as they opened the door to a white Chevrolet pickup truck and got in.

We were in business!

They maneuvered their truck through the parking lot exiting on the south side, where I happened to be waiting. They left the store parking lot and approached 10th street, the principal thoroughfare in McAllen, Texas. I was behind them with two cars between us. It occurred to me then that if they made me, they would turn my wife's Hello kitty car into Swiss cheese, with me in it. They turned south on 10th and then immediately turned into a car wash. I nearly panicked as they got out of the truck, as I didn't want to lose them. But I remained calm and drove past the car wash and pulled into a furniture store parking lot that gave me a perfect view of them.

Landin and one individual got into a four-door sedan parked near the exit of the car wash and waited as the other individual took care of business with the car wash. I watched patiently as the other guy emerged from the car wash and entered the sedan on the passenger side, with Landin seated in the back. It was at this point that I pulled out my Nextel and called my McAllen PD task force officer, Erik Torres, gave him the description of the suspect vehicle, and my wife's hello Kitty vehicle and told him to send me a unit immediately for a possible traffic stop. I could barely control my breathing as I spoke to Erik. I told him to keep it low profile because I wanted to make sure it was, in fact, Carlos Landin before letting anyone else know, especially the bosses in Houston.

When they left, the car was moving within the flow of traffic, going south on 10th street. I followed them cautiously for what seemed like an eternity. Erik called me and informed me that he had notified a unit in the area. Right after he said this, a McAllen PD unit pulled up alongside me and the officer gestured to me, as if asking which car. I pointed to the white four-door sedan, and he gave me a thumbs up and proceeded south on 10th behind the vehicle. Erik was in communication with the officer and gave me a play-by-play as the events developed. I dropped back and let the officer do his job. At the intersection of 10th and La Vista, the driver of the vehicle runs a red light, and the officer immediately pulls up behind him and flashes his emergency lights. The car with the three men pulled over, and I passed them up and pulled into an adjacent parking lot to watch the action.

The officer approached the vehicle, interacted with the occupants of the vehicle, and asked for their respective identification. My heart was pounding as I considered the magnitude of what was about to happen. The officer returns to his vehicle and calls Erik, who then calls me and says, "Leo, it's him. It's Carlos Landin Martinez! What do you want to do with him?"

"Get some more units to back up this officer and let's lock him up!"

Within minutes, the place was swarming with McAllen PD units, and I watched as they handcuffed Landin and put him in the back of a patrol unit. His life would never be the same. My next call was to Jimmy Bird. He genuinely thought I was fucking with him.

I told him, "Jimmy, call Erik and get all the details, then call the AUSA assigned to the case and let her know what just happened. We have a lot of work to do before Monday and no, I am not fucking with you. Now get off the phone so I can call the boss and let him know."

He let out a whooping victory cry before hanging up the phone.

So, I called my boss. He called his boss. And they called Washington, DC. Before dusk, the Administrator of the DEA was aware of what had transpired that Saturday afternoon in McAllen, Texas. I called our office in Monterrey to let them know. The rush of excitement swept through the whole agency like wildfire. I was taking and making calls all over the place, but there was one call I forgot to make in all the excitement. I forgot to call my wife and let her know I had gotten busy. She called me and when I saw the name on the incoming call list, my heart sank.

She had been worried sick, but I explained what happened and assured her I would be home soon. She understood. They always do.

Landin went to trial and on January of 2008, a jury of his peers found him guilty on 29 counts of charges ranging from Conspiracy to possess with the intent to distribute over 150 kilograms of cocaine, laundering over $1.5million in drug proceeds and possession with intent to distribute cocaine and marijuana. For these crimes, he received a sentenced of life in prison, where he died in December 2021.

So I revert to the question. Was it destiny or circumstance that brought us together?

All I know is that I did not wake up on the morning of July 14, intending or expecting to capture one of the most notorious members of the Gulf Cartel. I woke up expecting I would have a fun filled day with my family. I truly believe destiny truly brought us together on that summer afternoon in July, and I often wonder what would have happened if I hadn't gone to the store for corn at that specific time on that specific day. Why had I taken my wife's place? There is no logic or order to be found in it like so much in this world. Hell, his wife probably sent him out for a watermelon for a family gathering as well. Our paths crossed because of our love for and commitment to our families. Isn't that ironic?

I have always been curious what leads a man to a life of crime. In my research, I interviewed an old classmate of Landin's from Primaria Articulo 1, an elementary school in Reynosa Tamaulipas. The classmate told me that even as a kid, Landin had always been a bully, picking on weaker or smaller kids. The classmate recalled a time when, for no reason, Landin brutally beat on a much younger classmate in the playground, leaving him on the ground, bloodied and practically unconscious. Landin just laughed it off as if it were a big joke. As they got older, the classmate withdrew from Landin and the company he kept, stating that Landin never seemed to have any parental supervision and was always on his own, doing whatever he wanted to do. He drank alcohol at fourteen and avoided school altogether. So, from an early age, Landin lived a life of crime and violence, causing harm to others and had no remorse for it. He had to know that his life of crime would end someday—and it did, on that scorching hot summer day in July.

I did what I had to do, what I was trained to do, and what I love to do. I certainly don't have any regrets and never will.

Incineration of 2 tons of cocaine. Circa Feb 2003, Aguascalientes, Mexico

Carlos Landin-Martinez aka "El Puma". Booking photo taken shortly after his arrest.

Chapter 4: "El Canicon"

I had been in Monterrey almost a year already as the Resident Agent in Charge and the challenges we as a team face seemed insurmountable. In Northern Mexico, in the year 2008, significant changes occurred within the structure of the Gulf Cartel. The enforcement arm of the Gulf Cartel, Los Zetas, was striving to become independent, especially after the capture of the Gulf Cartel leader, Osiel Cardenas Guillen, who was in US Custody for his role in the attempted kidnapping of a DEA and FBI agent, as well as facing narcotics charges and operating a Continuing Criminal enterprise. After his capture, there was no apparent heir to the throne. Cardenas' longtime confidant, Jorge Eduardo Costilla aka "El Coss", was the de facto leader of the Gulf Cartel while in a parallel environment Heriberto Lazcano Lazcano, aka "El Lazca", was the leader of the Zetas. Lazcano's second in command was the most violent person in all of Mexico, Miguel Trevino-Morales, aka "Z-40". The vilest serial killers are on the kindergarten level compared to Trevino. Charles Manson is a choir boy compared to the atrocities committed by Trevino and the Zetas. After Osiel's arrest, the Zetas garnered more power and Lazcano took over the operational control of narcotics distribution for the organization. Costilla meanwhile took a hands-off approach and let Lazcano and Trevino take more operational control. This would prove to be a mistake, as the Zetas saw this as an opportunity to take control of the entire operation for themselves.

Osiel Cardenas Guillen recruited the Zetas, a team of former elite Special Forces soldiers from the Mexican Army who had either deserted or retired, to carry out assassinations on his behalf and to protect Cardenas himself from assassination. The move proved ingenious; One of the first members recruited by Cardenas was Arturo Guzman Decena, aka "Z-1", who was an explosives and intelligence expert. Cardenas, as most top-level narcotics bosses are, was extremely paranoid, and he tasked Guzman-Decena to recruit the best men possible for his personal security detail. This is how the Zetas originated. Guzman-Decena enticed active members as well as retired members of the Mexican military to join forces with him. The recruitment process was not difficult because active Mexican soldiers, even Special Forces soldiers, received paltry wages. The lure of more money and prestige allowed Guzman-Decena to recruit over thirty Special Forces soldiers with expertise in various departments such as explosives, intelligence gathering, communications, counter surveillance logistics and tactical combat. As a result, Cardenas amassed an elite team envied by other members of the Gulf Cartel and rival cartels as well. The team called themselves the Zetas, Spanish for the letter Z, as that was a common call sign for Mexican Special forces members.

When I arrived in Monterrey, the fracture between the two organizations was just starting. As a result of this imminent fracture, the Zetas started operating their own ventures across the Republic of Mexico, particularly in the Mexican states of Tamaulipas, Nuevo Leon, Coahuila, San Luis Potosi, Veracruz, Quintana Roo, and Zacatecas. The direct result of this fracture started a reign of terror throughout these states, specifically Tamaulipas and Nuevo Leon. The organization employed kidnappings, extortions, carjacking, armed assaults and robberies. In Nuevo Leon specifically, people were in denial. Most thought that the uptick in violence would pass after a certain period. However, the Zetas saw Nuevo Leon as a gold mine waiting to be exploited, especially in Monterrey and surrounding areas.

Monterrey is the third largest city in Mexico with a population of six million and is a major industrial center. It is home to prominent companies in sectors such as steel, cement, glass, and brewing and auto parts, and is also home to international companies such as Toshiba, John Deere, General Electric, KIA and Whirlpool, to name a few. San Pedro Garza Garcia, a suburb of Monterrey, boasts the most millionaires per capita in all of Latin America. Many people consider Monterrey to be a highly sophisticated cosmopolitan city with a thriving nightlife. An array of five-star restaurants and a variety of nightclubs beckons the populace to come and spend their hard-earned money.

In 2008, a sector in the downtown area of Monterrey known as El Barrio Antiguo was the most popular nighttime hangout. In the Historic Center of Monterrey, Barrio Antiguo offered first-class dining and entertainment for people of all ages. It was thriving. Business owners eagerly sought the opportunity to open a restaurant or bar in the sector, but all locales had already been taken and the rents were extremely expensive. Life was good for business owners in Barrio Antiguo, and Monterrey in general, until the wolf came knocking at the door. The wolf, or should I say a pack of wolves, appeared as the Zetas. Throughout this period, the Zetas showed formidable leadership and swiftly took advantage of the opportunities that came their way. The leaders of the Zetas were strategists and the only goal in mind was to make money and lots of it, no matter the cost. So, the Zetas ruled in Monterrey through then-Zeta Plaza Boss Sigifredo Najera-Talamantes alias El Canicon, playing out their strategy in Barrio Antiguo. A "plaza" is a region or territory assigned to a particular member of the leadership structure of Los Zetas. In this case, the Monterrey Region was a prime spot. The Regional Plaza Boss oversaw Zeta operations in cities or municipalities within the region, which in Monterrey were numerous and lucrative.

At first, they paid visits to the most successful nightclubs and demanded a weekly protection fee ranging in price from $5,000 to $10,000 US Dollars. Most business owners scoffed at the idea, but then received a second, more somber visit. On the second visit, the Zeta representative would arrive with pictures of the business owner's wife, children, or other family members, warning that failure to comply would lead to injury to either the owner or a family member. A failure to comply with the second request would cause immediate violence, whether it be in the form of a shooting inside the nightclub, a mysterious fire that destroyed the nightclub, or the nightclub owner actually getting kidnapped, tortured and sometimes murdered for failure to comply. Slowly, the Zetas began their takeover of Barrio Antiguo, saturating most of the nightclubs and restaurants with prostitutes, drugs, robbing and/or kidnapping customers at gunpoint in the sector. As a result, people stopped going, and many businesses closed their doors. It was just too dangerous to risk going there. The US Consulate warned their employees that Barrio Antiguo was a high-risk area and advised against going there at night.

I previously mentioned Sigifredo Najera-Talamantes alias El Canicon which translates literally into the "big Marble" as being the Zeta

Plaza Boss in Nuevo Leon. Canicon, as I will refer to him from now on, was the most trusted member of Zeta's second-in-command Miguel Trevino aka "Z-40". As such, Trevino placed him in charge of Monterrey, the most lucrative plaza in Northern Mexico, entrusting him to carry out the plan to wring the most money as possible out of the citizens of Monterrey. Canicon, although not having much of a formal education, was intelligent and used terror and fear as a tool to recruit local police officers, taxi drivers, waiters, waitresses, bartenders, and shoe shiners. The Zetas even recruited kids on the streets, to act as Canicon's eyes and ears throughout the city, alerting him to possible enforcement action by the military, Federal Police or to identify potential kidnap victims. He would also use them to sell drugs in bars or on the street. He had stash houses throughout the city where he kept his kidnap victims, sometimes protected by state and local police. He expected the people selling drugs for him on the street to meet a certain sales quota weekly. If the quota was not met, he would punish them by using a large piece of wood, simply called a tabla, to paddle their buttocks and hamstring area. A tabla is a piece of wood shaped like an oar for canoeing and is about 1.5 inches thick. It has holes perforated in the widest part to counter air resistance. The damage it inflicts is devastating. On that note, punishment for not meeting the quota was three tablazos. Punishment for stealing was over ten tablazos. If someone was caught stealing a second time, they would be punished with a slow and torturous death.

Our team in Monterrey interviewed many kidnap victims who were fortunate enough to get rescued from Canicon's grasp. One kidnap victim we interviewed described the terror he experienced in one of Canicon's stash/torture houses, a house he described as "La Casa del Infierno," the House of Hell. He had been kidnapped at gunpoint as he arrived at his office to start his workday. The victim, one of many millionaires from San Pedro, told us he was held in the House of Hell for about a week with at least twenty other victims. If one could smell fear, one could smell it in that house. Fear of the unknown, fear of death, fear of evil, fear-infused sweat permeated the house. Beatings were dealt out daily and they were all denied food and water for long periods of time. Not that anyone really had an appetite because some victims had urinated, vomited and defecated on themselves on the already blood-soaked floor, creating an unbelievably sickening stench that overpowered one's senses. The memory of this infernal stench made our victim gag for several minutes before regaining his composure and resuming his story. It was impossible to sleep with the fetid smell and the incessantly hopeless whimpering and cries for help from the other victims, earning more beatings and constant shouting by the Zetas ordering them to shut up and stop crying. Each passing minute seemed like an infinite lifetime. He said the Zetas took him into a room with about five other victims, and they immediately started severely beating one particular victim because his family had failed to pay the ransom within the required time frame. They pistol whipped the other four victims, including ours, and warned them that their respective families better pay the required ransom on time or they would be dismembered alive. "They hit me so hard that my left eardrum burst. I cannot hear out of my left ear anymore." He described how they left the person beaten in the room with him and the other victims to die a slow, agonizing death from the beating. "We were all blindfolded with duct tape, but we could hear this poor man gurgling, choking on his own blood, until we could hear him no more; while the Zetas merrily laughed it up as they raped one of the female victims in the house. I can still hear their diabolical laughter and the poor girl screaming in desperation and agony as they all took their turn with her. Hope did not exist in the House of Hell. An overwhelming feeling of immense horror, despair and gloom was engraved in our hearts, while we were in that house."

He told us that he also endured beatings with the infamous tabla and suffered four broken ribs. He managed to survive and share his story because his family paid over five million pesos for his release. They released him, naked, in a rural part of Cadereyta, Nuevo Leon. He would never forget how the Zetas who released him laughed at his nakedness and wondered in amusement how he was going to explain his nudity to his rescuers.

He said, "They fired shots into the air when they released me among whoops and hollers; I was in so much pain from my broken ribs; I really don't know how I managed to walk away after they dumped me on the side of the road. I realized that no matter how much money I had, my life meant nothing to these guys in that house. No amount of money was going to prevent the inferno I or the others would experience. To this day, it is impossible for me to sleep. I have to take medication just to sleep for maybe an hour, two if I am lucky. I will never ever forget the putrid smell. I can still hear the desperate pleading cries for help in the middle of the night, the savagely beaten man gurgling on his own blood and choking to death and the Zeta's satanic laughter as the poor girl screamed desperately for help, in a place where hope did not exist. Despues de sobrevivir la Casa del Infierno, mi vida nunca ha sido igual," which meant after surviving the House of Hell, my life has never been the same.

This is one minor example of the type of terror the Zetas unleashed in Monterrey. My coworkers and I frequently alluded to how the situation was like the flying monkeys in the Wizard of Oz terrorizing Dorothy and her companions and paralyzing them with fear. In this scenario, the flying monkeys were the Zetas, led by Trevino and Canicon, descending upon a helplessly unprepared and unsuspecting Monterrey populace.

The Zetas, at the height of their game, operated similarly to any sophisticated corporation. They had a CEO in Heriberto Lazcano-Lazcano who oversaw all Zeta operations in Mexico and the US. His executive assistant, Miguel Trevino, ensured his orders were carried out to the letter. The Zetas also had regional managers, called plaza bosses, who oversaw regions such as Northeastern Mexico, Southeastern Mexico, etc. These regional managers had subordinates who oversaw operations in each city. In Monterrey, there was a Plaza Boss in each suburb such as Guadalupe, San Nicolas, Escobedo, Cadereyta, Santa Catarina, etc. The local Plaza Bosses had their minions on the street selling drugs, identifying potential kidnap victims, committing robberies, carjackings, pushing pirated goods, pimping prostitutes, anything that generated money. At week's end, the local Plaza Bosses turned in their earnings to the local Zeta accountant, who turned over the earnings to a Regional accountant who reported to Trevino.

Unlike a conventional corporation, the management dealt with performance issues, discrepancies, or any form of insubordination violently. Any suspicion of malfeasance by an accountant, local Plaza Boss or minion was dealt with viciously, ranging on the low end from tablazos to the high end with severe and prolonged torture to death. The Zetas, especially Trevino and Canicon, were masters of torture. Witnesses interviewed recall that the Zetas, especially Trevino and Canicon, were masters of torture. They burned victims alive, skinned them alive, waterboarded them, or simply beat them to death with tablazos, usually in front of an audience of other Zetas. This served as an example to show that any performance issues or disloyalty would not be tolerated.

One of the many examples of Trevino's ruthlessness, in particular, caught our attention. One witness described how Trevino hunted down the alleged assassin of his brother and all conspirators that aided in the assassination of Trevino's brother. Most were beaten severely and then killed with a shot to the head. Trevino, however, saved his best work for the mastermind of his brother's killer. The victim, a Colombian national, had committed the murder at the behest of another trafficker named Edgar Valdez-Villarreal alias "La Barbie". Trevino had identified and kidnapped the victim's wife and infant child. With the victim subdued, Trevino made him watch as many Zetas savagely raped his wife, violated her with broomsticks, and eventually beat her to death. Trevino then took the victim's infant son who had his legs duct taped together, and a rope attached to the tape and legs, and held the child before his victim stating, "you have the balls to kill my brother, well watch as I kill your child." Trevino then took the child to a smoldering vat of oil and slowly dipped the child into the vat, alive. The witness described how he felt an extreme sense of terror as he watched Trevino, then laughed diabolically before killing the victim with a shot to the head. No one present during that scene ever dared cross Trevino again, and his mere presence made them tremble in fear, according to the witness. The story is incomprehensible to anyone with a conscience, and to this day still brings chills down my spine.

Another Trevino story told to us by a survivor of Trevino's psychotic mind games is just as unbelievably gruesome. In 2006, Trevino's girlfriend, with whom he was enamored, had grown tired of him and left him. Trevino, not being one to take rejection too well, has issues when people say no to him, was extremely upset at her decision. She thought nothing of it and decided to continue living her life as though nothing happened and eventually found another boyfriend of a more temperate nature. Trevino, however, was stewing with rage and vowed to find her and make her repent. The girlfriend, Maria, was living in San Antonio, TX to avoid Trevino. Her new boyfriend, however, was from Monterrey and he asked her to come down to Monterrey to visit him and asked her to bring a friend for his brother. With total disregard for her safety and the safety of her friend, Maria agreed and drove to Monterrey with her friend.

Upon arrival, they checked into the Crowne Plaza, on Avenida Constitucion, the main artery in the city near the Historic District. Little did they know the Zetas had spotted her as she entered the city and were actively following her. Maria and her friend checked into the hotel and eventually, her boyfriend and his brother picked them up. They had not gotten too far when they were all stopped at gunpoint by the Zetas, kidnapped and whisked away, the women to a safe house, and the men to a ranch. Trevino gave the Zeta in charge of the women the order to let Maria's friend go. But he mistakenly let Maria go and kept the friend in the stash house awaiting Trevino's arrival.

The victim, whom Trevino thought was Maria, was tied to a chair, her eyes and mouth wrapped in duct tape. When Trevino arrived and entered the room where the victim was being kept, he let out a diabolical laugh and said, "You thought you could get away from me! You thought you could outsmart me, right?" We will see who has the last laugh" Trevino dumped a bucket of cold water on the victim and violently cut off the tape from the victim's face. When the tape was removed, the victim describes how the look on Trevino's face changed from a confident smirk to confused, then enraged. He let out a savage yell and called for the man in charge of the woman. He showed the man a picture of Maria and repeatedly yelled, "This is not the one! How could you confuse them? Are you fucking stupid? They don't even look alike!"

The man, trembling with fear, became extremely apologetic and then began begging for his life. Trevino, breathing heavily with fury, pushed him away, and then coldly shot him in the head as if he was swatting a bothersome mosquito on a humid afternoon. The victim describes how the blood and brain matter splattered onto her face from her proximity to the man. She was so terrified she urinated on herself and was dry heaving from the fear of being killed herself.

Trevino approached her and put his face right into hers and practically hissed like a cobra; "I am going to show you something and I want you to send your little girlfriend a message! You are going to live tonight. But you must first see something!"

Trevino then called out to other Zetas and told them to blindfold the girl and take her to the ranch. He also ordered others to dispose of the dead man's body, saying, "Chop him up into pieces, burn him, do whatever, just get rid of him."

The Zetas tied her hands behind her back and blindfolded her with duct tape again and loaded her into a truck. The drive was long, and through what she described as rough terrain, for about an hour. She stated she was eventually unloaded, the blindfolds removed, and hands untied. Many armed men with ski masks occupied the ranch where they delivered her; somewhere in the distance, a bonfire was roaring and giving off a putrid smell. Masked, armed men led her to a clearing where several large cages were set up, with bright lights shining into them. She felt an overwhelming sense of fear and despair as she was led by numerous masked, armed men to a clearing. She started having trouble breathing when they reached the cages, where Trevino was waiting with a diabolical smile, the shadows of the roaring bonfire reflecting off his face.

Fearing what she would see, she closed her eyes. But the sounds and smells were frightening enough—as if a dog were crunching through a bone; the smell of raw meat and blood permeated the surrounding air. She said she didn't want to open her eyes, but Trevino grabbed her and told her again, "I want you to tell your little friend what you saw here tonight or else you will die right now! Open your fucking eyes and look." When she opened her eyes, she saw three Bengal tigers in the cage. Maria's boyfriend's head being devoured by one—the source of the crunching sound she'd heard was his skull being crushed by the tiger's powerful jaws. The other two tigers were busy devouring the body and head of his brother. Their blood soaked the tigers' fur. She heaved again but had nothing left in her stomach to throw up.

Trevino menacingly whispered into her ear, "Tell your little friend that I will find her; no matter where she tries to hide! And when I find her, she will meet a worse fate than her little boyfriend."

She could barely stand up and still thought Trevino was going to kill her, but Trevino ordered his men to: "Take the girl out of here and take her to the bus station." Trevino then turned back to her, smiled his diabolical smile, and said in parting; "Que Dios te bendiga mija," which means, God bless you, my child.

When I arrived in Monterrey, my mission was to target Miguel Trevino and all of his associates for apprehension, subsequent prosecution, and dismantle his organization. Trevino had just killed the commander of the Special Investigative Unit for all of Mexico. The commander had been a good friend of DEA's and I knew him personally, and the pressure was on to locate and apprehend Trevino. We were a team of four agents and one analyst in Monterrey. Although we were few, we were focused, determined, and driven. DEA had a big gun, and the gun was now focused on Miguel Trevino and his cohorts. The Monterrey office was chosen as the lead office in the hunt for Trevino and the Zetas.

We did what every DEA agent and office on a global level was trained to do, which is to learn as much as you can about your target and find his weakness, just like my longtime partner and confidante Mario Alvarez showed me early in my career. Our team put together a folder of photographs of Trevino and his family members and their family members, associates and every single report ever generated by DEA, FBI or ICE regarding Trevino. We had a war room plastered with photos of Trevino, Canicon, Lazcano and other members of the Gulf Cartel and Zetas all over the walls. All we needed now was some good actionable information on their activities or hangouts, stash houses, safe houses, and, most importantly, we needed a little luck.

As part of our strategy, we focused on the habits of our targets, locations they frequented, people they spoke to regularly. In the initial stages of the investigation, we received an overwhelming amount of information, which was a good thing. We mapped out locations of interest and got photographs of these locations for future use.

Then a significant incident took place that changed the dynamics of the game. On October 11, 2008, two grenades were launched at the US Consulate in Monterrey and the principal entrance to the building was fired upon multiple times during the late evening hours. One grenade detonated, causing damage to the front of the building. Fortunately, the attack took place after hours and the only people present were the security guards assigned to the building. The attack was unprecedented in Mexico. Never had a US Consulate been the subject of an attack by a Drug Trafficking organization.

The Law Enforcement Team at the US Consulate included DEA, ICE FBI, CIA and ATF along with the US Diplomatic Security Service. Although the attack occurred after hours, the probability of a follow up attack generated fear and panic in the US and Foreign Service Nationals employed at the Consulate. ATF requested an explosives expert to assist with the investigation, DEA Headquarters Special Operations Division sent an analyst and some agents to assist as well. The San Pedro Police department sent marked units and police officers to assist with security of the consulate. Although the Consulate had the support of the community, the attack took the community by surprise as well. The consensus was that if the US Consulate was the subject of an attack by this organization, and if the US Consulate was not immune to this type of intimidation, where did the public stand? The Zetas sent a clear message to the entire community that everyone and everybody was fair game, including the US Government. That was the biggest mistake that Trevino and Canicon could have made, because the attack united the US law enforcement community, who vowed that this act would not go unpunished.

Despite the vow, fear, tension and paranoia permeated the mindset of the Consulate community to the point of psychosis. People wanted answers and explanations, holding many meetings on the topic, and many of them were afraid to leave the Consulate for lunch or even a quick walk.

In this environment, the Law Enforcement Group went to work. We interviewed every single source we had at our disposal. In doing so, we discovered that a couple of weeks before the attack, Trevino's mother attempted to cross the border at the Laredo Texas port of entry. As I mentioned earlier, we had all of Trevino's family members identified and ICE flagged his mother as a person of interest. When she attempted to cross into the US, Customs and Border Patrol detained her for several hours, where she was questioned by ICE agents. This incident drew Trevino's ire, and he directed the attack on the US Consulate as retaliation for his mother's detention. The task was assigned to Canicon, the Monterrey Plaza Boss, who delegated the assignment to some lower-level Zetas. The two people who carried out the attack must have been extremely nervous because they tossed two grenades—one detonated, and the other didn't because they had not pulled the pin on the second grenade. We found the second grenade in the grass the following day. The façade of the consulate was shot nine times by a .45 caliber handgun.

We were actively tracking the movements of Canicon and Trevino, trying to determine a pattern of life, and we had developed a good pattern on Canicon. Based on our intelligence, we knew that Canicon frequently spent a significant portion of the early morning hours at a warehouse in downtown Monterrey. We had also located a house in Colonia Contry, where he seemed to bed down at night. This intelligence partnered with the intelligence received that Canicon orchestrated the attack on the Consulate, led the Law Enforcement team to hit both locations. Our Special Investigative Unit team, comprising of four Federal police officers who had been vetted by DEA, actively took part in every aspect of the investigation. However, hitting a warehouse as large as the one in question would necessitate the deployment of many reinforcements. So, our team requested the help of the Federal Police's Special Operations group or Grupo de Operaciones Especiales (GOPES). This marked the first time we used this group in a bilateral operation in Mexico. We briefed every entity and ensured everyone was on the same page; all we needed now was for Canicon to arrive at either of these two locations. Canicon's world was ready to come crashing down on him and his minions. The best part is, he didn't even know it.

Exactly three days after the attack on the Consulate, we were locked, loaded and ready to go. At approximately 1 AM, I got the call confirming that Canicon was at the warehouse, and I gave the green light to the team to hit the location. The darkness brought with it a combination of biting cold and relentless rain. After what seemed like an eternity, we got the call from the team leader advising that they had made entry into the warehouse and that they found a substantial amount of marijuana located there. He advised, with a nervous edge in his voice, that they would need reinforcements in case the Zetas attacked them to retake the warehouse. We solicited the help of the Army to assist our team and the GOPES to help safeguard the warehouse and were immediately sent reinforcements. The US Law Enforcement team immediately deployed to the scene of the warehouse to assist the team.

We were all pumped up with adrenaline as we drove down the eerily empty streets of downtown Monterrey. Luckily, the rain diminished to a tolerable level as we arrived at the warehouse. The first thing that caught our attention was that the media was already there in droves! We did not want the media to associate the search with the US Consulate, so we covered our diplomatic license plates with cardboard and tape so the media or curious onlookers would not identify us. The Army escorted us into the warehouse, where members of our team led us through the warehouse to the marijuana load. It was a trailer packed to the gills with marijuana, 9 tons to be exact, a crate containing 55 grenades, a trailer full of high speed DVD copiers and thousands of blank DVDs for recording movies or music for sale on the black market. Our explosive expert examined the crate of grenades and determined that the grenades used in the Consulate attack matched the lot number of the grenades found in Canicon's warehouse. We were ecstatic that we could directly link Canicon to the attack, but we still had business to attend to; We needed to capture Canicon and put him out of business.

Our intelligence showed that Canicon was now at the house, previously identified, in the Contry neighborhood. We now had three components to our team, the GOPES, the Army and our vetted team and we had to brief the Army as to the location of the house and the reputation Canicon had for violence. They decided to send all three components to the house to apprehend Canicon; we had discovered enough evidence to arrest him immediately.

Colonia Contry was about an hour away from our location. As much as we wanted to accompany the newly founded multi-agency team, my superiors in Mexico City ordered us to return to the Consulate, citing safety and potential sovereignty issues with the Government of Mexico. By this time, the media was already reporting on the seizure and we were getting calls from DEA Mexico City and DEA Headquarters in Washington, DC. My boss was in Monterrey because of the grenade attack and he had already reported the seizure to Washington DC and to the Regional Director of the North and

Central Americas Region. By the time we returned to the Consulate, the Administrator of DEA was already aware of the seizure.

Despite all this attention, we were more concerned about our team who were on their way to rock Canicon's world. We became more concerned when our team leader made a frantic call, stating that they were taking gunfire and one of our team members was wounded. We could hear the gunfire as our team member was requesting an ambulance. Upon receiving the report, we wasted no time and dispatched three ambulances to the scene, although they were quite reluctant to enter the war zone.

We were frantic ourselves; we had developed a close relationship with our team and the last thing we wanted was for someone to get hurt or killed. No sooner had we regrouped inside the Consulate to brief my boss, Assistant Regional Director Jose Baeza, when gunfire erupted outside the Consulate, and we knew it resulted from our actions earlier that morning. The chaos got worse when the Regional Security Officer (RSO) enacted the "duck and cover alarm" for the entire consulate. The signal for the alarm pierced the air and wailed like an unending ambulance siren. I immediately gave the order to our team to get the long weapons (AR-15s) and prepare to protect the US Consulate from further attack. In coordination with the RSO, the Law Enforcement Team took positions in different areas of the Consulate. In stark contrast to their previous paranoia and near-panic, I could not believe that some Consulate employees were walking around as if the alarm were a simple drill. We had to tell people forcefully to comply with the signal, that it was not a drill, and stay put until further notice.

Everything seemed to slow down for me, as if I were underwater. I yelled at a female Foreign Service National who seemed to be indifferent to the whole scenario, to duck and cover as I headed to my assigned section with two FBI agents. We did not know what to expect from the Zetas, considering the actions they had taken against the US Consulate a few days prior. We knew they could unleash holy hell with massive—firepower which we didn't have. Me and the two FBI agents were assigned to protect the principal entrance of the US Consulate, and I was the only agent in my team equipped with a long gun, while the FBI guys had handguns. We got to our assigned section, adrenaline running to the max, and we took up a tactical position. My friend and FBI companion became my eyes, and he immediately directed my attention to an individual at the street entrance to the Consulate. He was in his mid-thirties, wearing a dark jacket, and had his hands in his pockets. We were extremely concerned about another grenade being launched or the Zetas attacking the front gate with automatic weapon fire and using this individual as a distraction.

I focused on the individual's hands. My FBI counterpart repeatedly ordered the guy to show his hands, and he didn't comply. I had him in my sights, dead center of mass, just like our Firearms Instructor Steve Combs trained us to do in the Academy, ready to pull the trigger if he pulled a weapon or a grenade.

I felt as though I were floating in a bubble. My heart was pounding in my head and I could hear myself breathing. The individual then pulled his hands from within his jacket to reveal that they were empty. The man didn't realize that there was a high-powered rifle pointed at him, ready to end his life, as he stated he had a question regarding his Visa. An extreme sense of relief washed over me as he was instructed to leave the area and return at a later time.

After waiting for what seemed to be an hour, the duck and cover alarm was withdrawn, and we were ordered back to our offices. We followed up with our team leader and he informed us that none of our team members had been injured in the attack. He explained that when the team approached the house, they were met with immediate gunfire, to which they promptly responded. As the gunfight progressed, an armored vehicle with Canicon inside crashed through the garage door and escaped amidst a rain of gunfire. The team followed the fleeing vehicle to Avenida Constitucion, where it proceeded west before they lost it in traffic.

This piece of information confirmed for us that the shots fired at the Consulate came from Canicon and the Zetas. There had been over two hundred rounds exchanged and several grenades detonated between the Zetas and our team at the Contry house. The house was a typical flophouse, clothes strewn all over the place, empty beer cans, whiskey bottles and empty plates with old food littering the entire house. The kitchen floor was covered with fresh blood, indicating that our team had hit one, or possibly more, Zetas. The once quiet, quaint neighborhood had turned into a war zone. Stray gunfire had hit many houses and cars, neighbors cowered behind the doors of their houses, glad that the chaos had ended, but fearful and uncertain of what the future had in store for them.

The rest of the day was a blur as we had to attend several meetings regarding the events of the day, and report on our team's actions to Mexico City and Washington, DC. The media was in a frenzy over the events of the day. We had achieved our initial goal, which was to rattle the Zeta's cage and let them know that any aggression against the US Government would not go unpunished. He got away from us that day, but we were definitely not finished. Unfortunately, neither was Canicon. When I got home that day, my wife asked how my day had gone. With a smile, I said, "oh it was quite uneventful dear." I then opened a bottle of California Merlot and sat quietly, enjoying the mountain view from my patio while we listened to some smooth jazz as we watched the sun set on that adrenaline spiked day.

In the aftermath of the Consulate attack and our retaliation for it, we expected that a response by the Zetas was a reality. It could not only affect us, but our families as well. Our team made some security-based decisions that would counter or impede any attack, or at least give us a chance to escape without being injured in the event of an attack. The chief of police of San Pedro deployed two units to watch my house 24 hours a day. The same was done for the US Consul General. Our agents were provided with long arms to keep in our residences to defend ourselves in case of an attack.

After that day, fear and uncertainty became our constant companions, relentlessly permeating every facet of our daily lives. The worst part was knowing that this was only the beginning. We knew it would be only a matter of time before the Zetas struck again. The question was when and where? Time would soon tell us.

GOPES team raid Canicon's safehouse.
(Photo courtesy of Grupo-Reforma / El Norte)

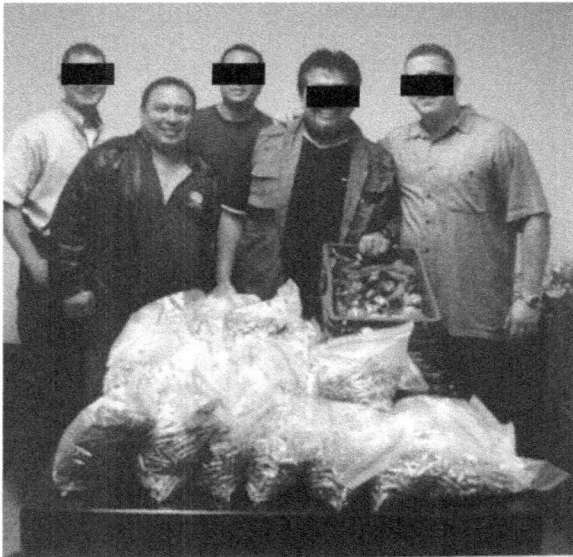

Leo Silva with the US Law Enforcement team at Canicon's warehouse, with stash of ammunition and grenade.

Official Zeta logo.
(Photo courtesy of Shutterstock.com)

Gold Zeta medallion awarded to Zetas who display courage and bravery.
(Photo courtesy of Getty images)

Chapter 5: "El Amarillo"

Canicon had luck on his side that morning and got away from us. But we were far from being done with him. But neither was he done with us. The operation's aftermath had basically left him broke and embarrassed in the eyes of Trevino and Lazcano, and he had to redeem himself. He sought that redemption by retaliating against the forces that shattered his world that day. The element of those forces that he retaliated on was the Mexican Army (SEDENA), which would prove to be another huge mistake for him and the Zetas.

After the raid, Canicon ordered his minions to stake out the military base located north of Monterrey in what is Escobedo, Nuevo Leon. The standing order was to kidnap any soldier who went on leave during the weekends. The military base is well-guarded but once one leaves, Zetas control the surrounding area. One can leave the base and go anywhere one pleases. However, the Zetas controlled all taxi traffic in the area. Whenever an unsuspecting soldier was picked up by a Zeta taxi, he was taken to a Zeta stash house, tortured and murdered by Canicon personally slitting his neck, and then dumped into the bed of the Rio Santa Catarina. Two of the soldiers who took part in the raid on the Contry house were among Canicon's victims. All in all, Canicon killed nine soldiers in this manner, at one point leaving a message on the body of one soldier. The message directed at the Army stating, "This is what happens when you fuck with the Zetas." Some soldiers had a Z carved into their backs, others on their foreheads. I saw photos of some of the dead soldiers, all young men in their early twenties, some of them already family men. The murder of these soldiers is referred to amongst the Mexican Army as Black October. These acts generated even more fear among the community. If soldiers could be picked up with such ease, how would the public deal with the threat? How could one protect one's family? These murders with the ongoing kidnappings, extortions, robberies and shootings created an oppressive environment of fear that permeated the lives of the citizens of Monterrey. The state and local authorities seemed to have no power to combat the issue. The citizens of Monterrey lived in a paralyzing world of Narco-violence.

Not too long after these incidents, our office received a call from the local Army base. The general in command of the 7th zone, who handled Monterrey and surrounding regions, wanted a meeting with our team. Subsequently, we scheduled a meeting and met with the General, a colonel, and intelligence analysts of the Army Special Forces team. On the day of the meeting, the Army held a special service in honor of the slain soldiers with the soldier's family members in attendance. We arrived after the service and immediately noticed the somber mood expressed by the General, the others in the meeting and the others in attendance. After exchanging brief pleasantries, the General got right to the point.

"Gentlemen, it is understood that all of us here at this table share a common enemy. I asked for your presence in this meeting because we share a common goal and the only way I see that goal being achieved is by uniting forces and sharing intelligence. My boss does not know that I called this meeting, but I don't care. What I care about is getting justice for the nine men that the Zetas killed. We will not rest until we have achieved that goal. I know you all have your motives, but I want you to understand mine. I am aware that in the past, our entities have not worked well together, but I think the time has come to change that mindset."

The request surprised and excited us. To my knowledge, no DEA office in Mexico had an everyday working relationship with the Army. I responded for the group, "General, we are willing to do whatever it takes to bring justice to the memory of your men. You can count on us to support you and your group with anything we can."

The General explained to us that the group would be close knit and only certain personnel would be privy to our newfound relationship. The general and the Colonel had selected an elite group of Special Forces analysts and operatives to work hand in hand with us exclusively. It was another significant relationship that our team had developed to attack the Zetas. We now had the GOPES and the Army Special Forces in our corner, in this seemingly impossible war against the Zetas and organized crime in Mexico, and we were prepared to put an end to Canicon's reign of terror in Monterrey.

But there was someone else who we were tracking—someone who required our immediate attention. Canicon may have been a major focus, but he wasn't the only focus.

The Gulf Cartel and the Zetas worked in a parallel environment. Therefore, both factions had their own leadership structure. In the city of Reynosa Tamaulipas, the leader for the Gulf Cartel was Antonio Galarza Coronado, aka "El Amarillo". On Zeta's side of this formula, the leader was Jaime Gonzalez Duran aka "El Hummer". These names would come to increased prominence in the coming weeks.

Our team was informed that "El Amarillo," referred to as "the yellow one," would make an appearance in Monterrey after the Canicon operation. Their purpose was to meet with organization members and uncover the truth behind the Canicon incident. Our source advised that after the meeting, Amarillo would go to a local restaurant to grab a quick bite to eat before he made the two-hour trip north to Reynosa. We saw it as a golden opportunity to arrest him, as well. We advised our team about the situation, however we had received the information late and the GOPES could not make it in time to conduct an arrest operation on Amarillo. Without this crucial member of the team, we opted to surveil the restaurant where he would eat and develop more intelligence on his patterns and habits.

Three of us, including one member of our vetted team, locked and loaded our AR-15s, piled into our armored Suburban and headed out towards La Carretera Nacional, east of Monterrey, to the city of Santiago. El Amarillo had picked Restaurant Garcia, a restaurant famous for its dried beef or "machacado" as it is called in Spanish. Although we were there strictly for intelligence, we were still mindful that we were dealing with the Gulf Cartel and Los Zetas, who we had just shaken up in a big way, so we were heavily armed. If the Zetas were to take notice of our diplomatic tags, they would have stopped us immediately to investigate our reason for being there, and who knows what would have happened then? We knew we were breaking the rules by going out on the street so heavily armed, but we would not allow ourselves to be killed because we followed the rules.

We set up our surveillance on the side of the road near a pottery shop that was situated across the street from the restaurant, giving us a clear view of the parking lot. One of our guys actually went into the pottery shop to give the impression that he was shopping while the rest of us stayed in the car and waited for "El Amarillo" to arrive. It wasn't long before he pulled up in a brand new black Ford Lobo, worthy of a Gulf Cartel Plaza Boss. He went into the restaurant and after about an hour, he left. We followed him for a short distance to a busy intersection. There, he made a sharp turn, headed through a grocery store parking lot and then zipped out onto the highway, leaving us stuck at the light with traffic all around us. In a matter of minutes, he had escaped our surveillance. Next time, we would have to do a much better job if we were going to get him. We considered that surveillance as a dry run for the real thing, and assessed lessons learned.

The challenge we faced that day was the limited resources—only one vehicle—as we attempted to follow Amarillo. Next time, we would need several vehicles to avoid losing him in traffic. We went to work and got the GOPES on board for the next operation, which we figured would be the following week based on the information provided by our source. In the meantime, we traveled out to the same restaurant and studied the layout of the area, looking for strategic points that we could use to place a surveillance vehicle, and identify potential counter surveillance points that the Zetas could use to identify us. Amarillo was a Plaza Boss with abundant resources, and we were cautious not to underestimate him. We wanted to be sure we had every base covered, every potential escape route covered, so he didn't escape, as Canicon had.

Our team was fired up to get on with the mission, as we anxiously waited for the source to call us and let us know when Amarillo would visit Monterrey again. We got our break on October 30, 2008, exactly sixteen days after our attempt to apprehend Canicon. Our source told us that Amarillo would come into town in the afternoon and would stop at the same restaurant as before. We were ecstatic that he had chosen the same restaurant. This told us he felt comfortable there and had not spotted our surveillance the last time he was there. If he had spotted us, he would not have returned to the same place. So, we locked and loaded again. And this time we would not be alone.

We had our entire vetted unit and a team of fifteen GOPES, all ready for action.

Our plan was simple. We would act as the surveillance point on Amarillo at the restaurant and we were to call out his direction of travel to our vetted team and GOPES as he left the restaurant. The vetted team and GOPES were to remain hidden from view at an area we had identified during our recon missions. Once the team and GOPES got visual surveillance on Amarillo, they would box him in with their vehicles and effect his arrest. Once the stop was made, we were assigned to serve as back up, in case the Zetas attempted to ambush the arrest team and rescue Amarillo. The mission had the potential for a big firefight, but we were ready. The two agents with me and I vowed not be taken alive by the Zetas to be tortured mercilessly. We were prepared to fight down to our last round of ammunition if needed. And just in case we ran out of ammunition, we each had a five-inch combat knife we were prepared to use on any would be attacker if it got to that point. With these dark thoughts on our mind and charged up with adrenaline, we silently drove out to Santiago to initiate the operation.

Dusk was falling as we arrived in Santiago. We took up our surveillance spot on the restaurant and waited for Amarillo's arrival. There was an eerie calm on the crisp October evening as the patrons went in and out of the restaurant, oblivious to the events about to unfold around them. We decided to arrest Amarillo away from the restaurant. He would be most vulnerable in his vehicle on the road, and more importantly, in case a firefight broke out, we did not want innocent bystanders to get hurt or killed by stray gunfire.

At around 7:00 PM, the black Ford Lobo pulled into the restaurant parking lot.

"Showtime boys!" I said as I checked my AR-15 one more time.

We called our vetted team and told them to get ready as we waited for Amarillo to finish his business at the restaurant. The only difference from last time is that an unknown male accompanied him. Traditionally in Mexico, lunches and dinners are not quick thirty-minute meals, and usually lasted up to two hours. So, after waiting for about an hour, we were pleasantly surprised to see Amarillo and his friend exit the restaurant, get into their vehicle, and drive off.

The game was on now!

Amarillo went east, took a loop and came back west, passing our vehicle on the driver's side. We called out his direction of travel to the vetted team. Once he had traveled a short distance, we started following him. We did not want to spook him and knew from the last attempt he was proficient in counter-surveillance maneuvers. We followed him to the same intersection as before and, luckily for us, he did not attempt the same move, although he probably could have lost us again had he done so.

The traffic was heavy, as people were trying to make their way home from work. We were practically on his bumper and he was the first vehicle at the red light. In the meantime, our vetted team called us and told us they were stuck in traffic and trying to make their way out to the main highway to join us. Suddenly and much to our surprise Amarillo gunned his vehicle in the middle of traffic and blew the red light, leaving us back at the intersection stuck in traffic. It was a classic counter surveillance move. As he sped away, he turned into an H-E-B grocery store parking lot and disappeared from view, we watched in dismay. Upon alerting the vetted team and GOPES about the situation, they began scouring the area to locate Amarillo, but he was nowhere to be found. We fretfully searched all the potential hiding spots we had previously identified, but nothing turned up. He had vanished.

We were about to give up when we got a call from our source. "He knows you all are following him." He said. "Are you all in blue suburban?"

"Yes," replied my partner.

"Well, he made you and he is calling for reinforcement right now to track you down. You best get out of there."

"Wait, is he still in the area?"

"Let me check on it and I will call you back, but you better get out of there now!"

My heart started pounding as the thought of a potential shootout with the Zetas now became real. We called our vetted team and informed them we had been made and Zeta reinforcements were on the way. In case they were watching us, we met up to show that we were not alone and had reinforcements as well.

Everything was surreal and chaotic. We, the hunters, had now become the hunted, and we rapidly tried to develop a strategy to leave the area.

The source called us back and told us that Amarillo was still in the area waiting for the reinforcements to arrive and that some Zeta scouts had already spotted us meeting with our vetted team. Shit was going to hit the fan soon if we did not get out of there fast. According to the source, El Amarillo was waiting in the hospital parking lot, which was located across the street from the H-E-B where our vetted team had gathered.

Time was of the essence. I could practically hear the seconds ticking away in my head.

Our strategy was to leave the area with our vetted team following us and the GOPES leading the way with their marked vehicles, lights flashing and all. The GOPES advised they were on the highway west bound, just coming up on the H-E-B parking lot ready to lead the way for us.

But things were moving fast.

The hospital where Amarillo was waiting was within sight of the GOPES. Our vetted commander informed the GOPES of Amarillo's potential location, and they advised they would check on it. We started moving. Our vetted team followed us as we slowly made our way out of the parking lot. As soon as we reached the highway to turn west, we received a call from the GOPES.

"We got him!"

We let out triumphant roars and celebrated by exchanging high-fives so hard our hands stung from the impact. But any more celebration than that was premature.

The potential for a rescue attempt was still front and center in our minds. So, the GOPES quickly threw Amarillo and his friend into their marked vehicle and rushed out of there, hauling them away to the military base. The rescue attempt never materialized, and our vetted team escorted us back to the Consulate.

As we reached the Consulate grounds, a wave of relief washed over us. We learned that Amarillo and his buddy had two fragmentation grenades and two forty-five caliber pistols in their possession and things could have gone much worse. But our tasks were far from over.

We wanted to interview Amarillo, but that meant we had to get to the Army base.

At the Consulate, we changed vehicles and started on our way to the military base when we got a call from the Federal Police commander. He told us not to go to the military base because the Zetas were already watching the base, waiting for an opportunity to rescue Amarillo and to see who went in and out of the base. They had already called the base and issued threats of violence if Amarillo was not released. But, after the brutality that Canicon had inflicted on played on the Army's troops in Black October, there was no chance that they were going to give in to the demands of the Zetas. In fact, they welcomed any potential violent response and were ready for anything.

Not wanting to give the Zetas another reason to attack the US Consulate or, worse yet, one of our employees. We took the commander's advice and decided not to go. Instead, we had a celebratory round of beers and saluted Team USA's latest victory against the Gulf Cartel and the Zetas—and that we had made it out in one piece.

However, we knew things were just starting to heat up and that the fight had just begun.

Chapter 6: "El Hummer"

At the time we began the investigation on the Zetas, specifically Canicon and Trevino, we developed extremely reliable information regarding another Zeta Plaza Boss, Jaime Gonzalez-Duran, aka "El Hummer", who was the Reynosa Plaza Boss. Reynosa Tamaulipas, Mexico, is on the border with South Texas specifically Hidalgo and McAllen, Texas and is one of the most strategic areas for narcotic smuggling. The Reynosa Plaza is a gateway to the Northern United States cities, where profits immediately double once the drugs make it into the US. For example, a pound of marijuana that costs 25 dollars a pound in Mexico costs 60 dollars a pound in McAllen. Once taken north of the checkpoint, the cost rises to 200 dollars a pound, but in northern cities such as Chicago or New York the price goes up to almost 500 dollars a pound. Huge profit margin. However, the profit margin for cocaine, crystal meth and heroin was even higher! The Gulf Cartel controlled the Reynosa Plaza, but they allowed other cartels to smuggle their shipments for a fee paid to the Gulf Cartel. In conjunction, DEA McAllen, DEA Matamoros, FBI and DEA Monterrey briefed a Special Forces commander from the Mexican Army to get them to conduct an operation on El Hummer.

The commander was part of the CIA's vetted team and commanded an elite squadron of soldiers, exactly what we needed for an operation against Hummer. Hummer, like Canicon, was an extremely dangerous and violent person. An original Zeta, he was a former Army Special Forces member and was an expert at counter insurgency and intelligence. After his stint in the Army, he served in the office of Procuraduria General de La Republica (PGR) in Reynosa, Tamulipas, the equivalent of the Attorney General's office. He was widely considered the mastermind behind the assassination in Reynosa of a popular Mexican singer, Valentin Elizalde in 2007.

Valentin Elizalde was a native of Sinaloa Mexico, home of the Sinaloa Cartel, mortal rival of the Gulf Cartel. Elizalde sang songs praising the narco bosses of his home town of Culiacan, Sinaloa, territory of the notorious Chapo Guzman. When he went to perform in Reynosa Tamaulipas, the Gulf Cartel warned him not to sing a particular song that offended the Gulf Cartel. The song was "Para todos mis enemigos," (For all my enemies). He defied the order and sang the song to finish his show. No sooner did he finish his concert and leave the stage for the airport than someone assassinated him and his driver. Shot many times by a high-powered weapon, an AK-47.

Besides this act of violence and in the wake of the Canicon operation, "El Hummer" issued a directive to the Zetas who operated in McAllen, TX and surrounding areas to attack any US Law enforcement agents who intervened or attempted to intervene with the operations of the Zetas and Gulf Cartel. This order definitely caught our attention and proved to be a tactical error on Hummer's part.

From September to October, we briefed the commander and his boss numerous times, even letting them interview one of our sources of information to determine his veracity. They seemed non-committal and unwilling to act on the information. It was an extremely frustrating effort. This team was supposed to be the most elite team in Mexico, but they did not want to take action. We were practically giving Hummer to them on a silver platter, but they always came back and told us they needed more information. Feeling helpless, angry, and frustrated, we reevaluated our options. With the success we had with the GOPES on the Canicon and Amarillo operations, each office decided to use the GOPES to conduct a similar enforcement operation and avoid the Army Special Forces.

On November 7, 2008, almost one month after the Canicon operation, the GOPES geared up to take down Hummer, one of the most feared Plaza Bosses, within the Zeta organization. We decided that the team's presence in Reynosa would attract too much attention, so they spent the nights prior to the operation in McAllen, TX, going over the details repeatedly.

We had collectively decided that the GOPES should rent unmarked vehicles, to not attract attention to themselves and compromise the operation. On the morning of November 7, 2008, the GOPES set up surveillance on two locations identified as being most frequented by Hummer: named simply as location A and location B. When it was determined that Hummer was at location A, the GOPES moved in undetected and hit the house full force. It was a moment of chaos as they searched the house thoroughly, finding numerous high-powered weapons. But Hummer was nowhere in sight.

DEA exchanged many calls with the GOPES, advising the GOPES that there was no way Hummer could not be in the house—he did not have magical powers that would render him invisible. The GOPES searched again and this time found him cowering under two single beds that had been pulled together and covered with a blanket. I found it funny that this big time Plaza Boss, who invoked fear in the hearts of hardened criminals, was wracked with fear and cowering under a bed, like a kid playing hide and seek with his mommy. He carried a gold plated .38 Special but lacked the courage or time to use it. It's all fun and games until you are the target and your bodyguards aren't around to save your ass. The GOPES took him into custody but immediately faced another dilemma. Hummer had managed to send an alert to his Zeta cohorts that he was being taken into custody, and the Zetas took immediate actions. They responded by making an all-out effort to rescue their boss from arrest. They created obstacles in major thoroughfares with burning tires; blockades with urban buses and tractor trailers; They stole vehicles at gunpoint from innocent citizens, burning them in the streets to create more traffic congestion and turmoil, turning Reynosa into an urban war zone. The Zetas aggressively pursued the GOPES, in a high speed chase throughout the city, engaging them in an ongoing shootout with high-powered weapons and launching fragmentation grenades at their vehicles. The GOPES skillfully sped through the city amid the gunfire, explosions and roadblocks, whisking Hummer away to a Federal Police aircraft, waiting at the Reynosa airport.

My counterpart in Matamoros recalls the commander of the GOPES calling him and advising, "we have him; we are taking gunfire but they will take him over my dead body," as they made their way to the airport. My counterpart advised he could hear the gunfire as he spoke to the commander, who was jacked up on adrenaline, shouting into the phone. After a prolonged gun battle, they loaded Hummer onto the Federal Police jet and sent him directly to Mexico City, far away from Reynosa and his duties as a Zeta Plaza boss. He had gone to sleep the prior evening as the Plaza boss of one of the most important regions in Mexico and the following evening was incarcerated in a jail cell in Mexico City with only the clothes on his back. He is still incarcerated there, awaiting extradition to the United States. The operation resulted in the largest weapons seizure in Mexico: over 500 rifles, 168 grenades, 7 Barret .50 caliber rifles,14 cartridges of dynamite, several grenade launchers and over 500,000 rounds of ammunition. Also seized was approximately 1 million pesos, the equivalent of approximately $100,000 in cash. Fortunately, none of the GOPES were injured in the gun battle.

In a couple of weeks, we successfully conducted operations on three high profile Zeta Plaza Bosses. We had hurt them and created a vacuum of leadership within the Northeast Mexico Zeta and Gulf cartel structure. The beauty of it was that we had also created doubt within the organization, as they did not know where the information was coming from. They felt baffled, dumbfounded, and enraged.

A dangerous combination of emotions.

It was not over between Trevino, Canicon and Law Enforcement entities. Our plan was to keep applying the pressure until we captured Trevino and Lazcano and put the Zetas out of business.

El Hummer is presented to the media by GOPES team.
(Photo courtesy of Grupo Reforma / El Norte)

Chapter 7: Rocking and Rolling

After the operations on Canicon, Amarillo, and Hummer, we regrouped as the holidays were approaching. yet we wanted to keep applying the pressure on the Zetas. We thought in order to get to Trevino and Lazcano, we must attack their leadership structure not only in Monterrey and Tamaulipas, but in all of Mexico. The GOPES were red hot, and we intended to keep using them for our operations. Our new friendship with the Army was also proving to be effective as they were gathering valuable information on different members of the Zetas in Nuevo Leon. They were eager to seek revenge for their fallen comrades.

In late November, we received intelligence that Lazcano was at a ranch in the State of San Luis Potosi. Rancho El Atoron, as it was known, was in Santa Maria del Rio in San Luis Potosi. It is located 1700 meters above sea level and lies on the western edge of the Sierra Madre Oriental. It was rough, mountainous terrain out there, and it would be difficult to conduct an enforcement operation without alerting Lazcano and his security circle to the presence of the arrest team. We knew Lazcano loved the outdoors and enjoyed hunting exotic game on many of his ranches; we just never knew where these ranches were located, but we now had a fix on one of them.

As the leader of the Zetas, Lazcano, known as Z-3, usually had a circle of over thirty bodyguards surrounding him, but we also knew that he liked to travel alone and incognito or with a smaller group, in order to avoid drawing attention to himself. However, we had no way of knowing how big a group would be with him at the ranch. This presented us with a major predicament, because we did not want to send the arrest team into a gunfight where they would be out-manned and outgunned. This was also an opportunity to immediately cripple the Zetas organization severely by capturing their leader. So, despite the risks, the decision was made to go forward with the operation and attempt to capture Lazcano.

My bosses in Mexico City made the decision. This was not an issue, but giving operational control to an agent in Mexico City was problematic. The agent in control decided to use the Army Special Forces unit that did not cooperate with us on the Hummer mission. They made these decisions without informing me, and on the eve of the operation, the Army, as they had done so many times during the Hummer operation, chose not to participate, causing a frantic scramble to involve the GOPES. Finally, on December 5, 2008, at 6:00 am, the GOPES swooped in on Rancho El Atoron, with two helicopters and two assault teams, but Lazcano was nowhere to be found.

The GOPES arrested four individuals, including two highly trusted members of Lazcano's circle, Victor Hugo Lopez Valdez, aka "El Chiricuas", and Pablo Gomez Solanos, aka "El Paguas". The other defendants were merely ranch hands and not members of the Zetas. We would later learn that Lazcano had been at the ranch and escaped when he heard the thumping of the helicopter rotors and had fled into the mountainous brush land. He survived for three days without food or water before Miguel Trevino rescued him. We would also learn that the Plaza Boss for San Luis Potosi "El Peter" escaped with

Lazcano, only to fall off a cliff and die from his injuries. The GOPES found his broken body as they tried to hunt Lazcano down in the cragged terrain. They also found in the ranch house numerous recent photographs of Lazcano in several locations on his many hunting expeditions. Some of those pictures were disturbing, including one of "El Chiricuas," showing off with a Zebra he had killed, and several of Lazcano posing with exotic gazelles, zebras and mountain lions.

After being rescued, Lazcano was sick with fury and immediately ordered the execution of all persons who were aware of his presence at the ranch and had not been arrested. Also, after the arrest and before Christmas, the Zetas decapitated a dozen soldiers in Chilpancingo Guerrero and lined them up in a high traffic area with a sign that read "For every one of mine that you kill, I will kill ten of yours!" Near the bodies, authorities found a sack containing the heads of the victims, some of whom were still gagged with tape.

We are not sure whether the murders were related to the operation on Lazcano, but in this business, coincidences are few and far between. The team and I were furious about being cut out of the deal, but we were excited about challenging Lazcano. We had come close this time and shaken him up. He was now on notice that he was not untouchable. We had the full attention of Trevino and Lazcano.

From that day on, they knew we were a force to be reckoned with.

The holidays came and went, and the New Year started off with a bang—literally. On January 5, 2009, the Zetas attacked the television station, Televisa, by launching a grenade into the parking lot and firing approximately fifteen nine-millimeter rounds into the façade of the building, causing panic and hysteria among the employees. Fortunately, no one was injured in the attack, but some people suffered anxiety attacks and had to be attended to by paramedics who arrived at the scene. The Zetas left a message written on a poster board at the scene which read "Stop transmitting news only about us! Transmit news about the corrupt officials too!"

Nuevo Leon State officials called members of the US Law Enforcement Team and we immediately responded to the scene. There was not much we could do then, but it was clear that the Zetas were ready to take on anyone who appeared to stand in their way—there was no end to the level of violent measures the Zetas were willing to take. The way we saw it, Canicon and the Zetas had attacked the US Consulate, killed nine Mexican Army officials in Nuevo Leon, twelve in Guerrero and had now attacked the most powerful television station in Mexico, among other atrocities. They were highly unpredictable and, above all, fearless. The only way to meet strength was with strength—we had to show them their tactics would not intimidate us and that we would stand toe to toe with them.

To do this, we implemented a strategy designed to take down not only the leadership structure of the Zetas but also all remaining original Zetas members recruited by Arturo Guzman Decena. We started with Miguel Angel Soto Parra, aka "El Parras," or "El Dalmato." He was an original Zeta, and ex-member of the Mexican Army, who at one time had been a member of the Mexican Federal Judicial Police in Tamaulipas and served as one of Osiel Cardenas Guillen's personal bodyguards. He had gone underground, but we received intelligence that he was living in Mexico City.

We provided the information to the GOPES and exactly three days after the Televisa attack, the authorities took "El Parras" into custody in Colonia Villas de Coyoacan, in Mexico City. He gave up without a shot being fired.

The fight was on. We were in the ring, going toe to toe with the Zetas. The best part of the whole thing is that we were creating doubt in their psyche—they did not know where we were getting the information to hit them so hard and effectively.

When a member of the Zetas or Gulf Cartel gets killed or captured, he is replaced immediately. After "El Hummer's" arrest in Reynosa, Hector Saucedo Gamboa, aka "El Karis," filled the void.

Let me offer a brief history on "El Karis:" When Osiel Cardenas Guillen was in power, one of his trusted associates, Gregorio Sauce-da-Gamboa, aka "El Goyo," was in charge of the Reynosa Plaza. "El Goyo" operated the Plaza efficiently and with a heavy hand, ensuring that every penny owed to the Gulf Cartel was paid and paid on time. El Karis, the younger brother of "El Goyo," operated in the Nuevo Laredo Plaza, assisting the Zetas in eliminating members of the Sinaloa Cartel who wanted to operate in the area. El Goyo, meanwhile, started getting sloppy and suffered health problems because of an addiction to cocaine. His addiction was interfering with his ability to operate effectively. They replaced him and banished him to his hometown of Matamoros, Tamaulipas.

After the high-profile arrests of "El Hummer." and "El Amarillo," "El Karis" moved in to take over the Plaza, but El Karis' loyalties were with the Gulf Cartel, and he hated Miguel Trevino with a passion. "El Karis" was impulsive, had an explosive temper, was not mentally stable and frequently clashed with Zetas assigned to the Plaza. He even vowed to eliminate Trevino himself, at times. Conflicts such as these added fire to the already brewing feud between the Zetas and the Gulf cartel.

On February 17, 2009, at approximately 11:00 am, members of the Army, while patrolling the streets of Reynosa, happened upon Karis' convoy of vehicles. Like something out of an action movie, a gunfight erupted and once again turned the city of Reynosa into a war zone. Karis and company attempted to flee from the soldiers, firing their automatic weapons at them as they fled through the city's streets, much to the horror of innocent bystanders going about their daily activities. The Army responded with heavy automatic gunfire and grenade launchers. The Federal Police also joined the fray as Karis' convoy split up and sped through the streets of the city, both factions firing thousands of rounds in the pursuit.

Unbeknownst to Karis and the Gulf Cartel, the Zetas had planned an attack on Karis on the same day and also joined in the firefight. The Zetas commandeered city buses and tractor trailers, forcing citizens out of their vehicles and using them to block strategic avenues throughout the city and preventing reinforcements from the Federal police or Army to assist in the firefight. Several buses and vehicles were set on fire. A torrential rain of gunfire, terror, and chaos raged throughout the city for two hours. When the shooting finally stopped, twenty bullet-riddled bodies lay throughout the streets of Reynosa, including Karis and his personal bodyguard. Residents of Reynosa, however, reported that the body count was much higher than what was being reported in the press. Some residents saw Gulf Cartel and Zeta members loading dead bodies into the beds of pickup trucks and driving away, so the actual body count would remain unknown. Besides those involved, unfortunately, the gun-battle wounded some innocent bystanders as well.

On the surface, this incident appears to be a gunfight that erupted between Karis and his men and the Army and the Federal Police. What it was, however, was a well-planned and coordinated attack by the Zetas on Karis.

On that day, while the gun battle raged on the streets of Reynosa, protesters throughout the entire country showed up in droves to protest military action. These protests led to the shut down of eight ports of entry to the United States, including the Reynosa-Hidalgo Port of Entry, Pharr-Hidalgo Port of Entry, the Brownsville-Matamoros port of entry, Juarez Lincoln Port of Entry, and the Free Trade port of entry in Laredo, as well as three Ports of Entry in Ciudad Juarez. In typical Zeta mode, the protesters used tractor trailers, hijacked buses and vehicles to block bridge traffic. They burned tires and trash in the streets, hurled rocks at soldiers, broke store and vehicle windows and terrorized innocent citizens. These blockades lasted for over five hours, severely disrupting trade and other daily border activities. Protesters also showed up by the busload in Monterrey, Ciudad Victoria Ciudad Juarez and Vera Cruz to protest military presence and actions.

In Monterrey, the blockades generated fear throughout the US Consulate as employees feared getting attacked again. The blockades caused traffic to come to a standstill for hours in Monterrey, and we were essentially trapped inside the Consulate, hoping and praying that we would not face another attack. Many of us, including me, whose spouses did not work at the Consulate were frantic to get home and protect our families, but we could go nowhere.

As I mentioned before, the Zetas were former Special Forces soldiers and many of them were experts at counter insurgency and we witnessed firsthand the reach of their expertise in counter insurgency and psychological warfare. The Zetas gave out back packs filled with school supplies and paid 300 pesos to women, teenagers, taxi drivers, shoe shiners, and others with low economic resources to assist in the protests. In Monterrey, these folks were in abundance. The Zetas even brought sandwiches and soft drinks to the many protesters in Laredo to sustain them during their efforts. Besides disrupting traffic and creating terror throughout the country, the protests served as the perfect cover for the Zetas to move into Reynosa to carry out the attack on Karis.

It was a brilliant plan. The Zetas, however, didn't plan on the Army and Federal Police beating them to the punch and engaging Karis first. Karis' death was not an operation that was planned out by our team, but Lazcano and Trevino did not know that. All they knew is that they had just been beaten to the punch and they were pissed. All we cared about was that another member of their leadership structure had been eliminated. It was a silver lining to the dark cloud left by the protesters who basically held Monterrey hostage that whole week, eventually clashing with severely under-manned and under equipped state and local authorities and killing a state police investigator who had arrested one of the protest leaders.

It was a foreboding era for the citizens of Monterrey and employees of the US Consulate. Unfortunately, it was only the beginning of a long, dark journey.

Chapter 8: Justice

February had been a stressful month, but we needed to move forward with our plan. DEA Headquarters provided us with support, sending a staff coordinator from the Special Operations Division and OTP, along with an analyst, to assist with the operations against Lazcano, Trevino, and Canicon. Having DEA headquarters personnel in town was highly beneficial, streamlining the process of reaching out to DEA headquarters in Washington DC, securing funding or analytic support, and avoiding lengthy delays in receiving a response. Having them in Monterrey with us meant we had on-the-spot support whenever we needed it. Their presence also helped us out with manpower issues.

We had a lot of work and we needed all the manpower we could get. There were four crucial leads that required immediate follow-up. Our Army counterparts had developed information that Canicon was now operating out of Saltillo, Coahuila. They also had developed information on a ranch house that was being used by Miguel Trevino, which was surprisingly located near the Army base. They also had actionable information on one leader of the Beltran-Leyva organization, Hector Huerta, aka "La Burra." Huerta held the position of the Plaza Boss for the Beltran-Leyva organization in Monterrey and also served as the liaison between the Zetas and the Beltran-Leyva organization, led by Arturo Beltran Leyva. At the same time, our team had developed information on another Zeta Plaza Boss, Sergio Pena Mendoza aka "El Concord." All four targets were options for an operation. We would have to plan carefully for each one and execute the operations in three phases.

"El Concord" was the next man up after the arrests of El Hummer, El Amarillo and the death of El Karis. El Concord had established himself as a worthy member of the Zetas organization, in spite of the fact that he was not an original Zeta. El Concord was likely recruited into the Zetas organization by Jaime Gonzalez Duran, "El Hummer." El Concord's criminal history dates back to 2003, when authorities arrested him in Nuevo Laredo Tamaulipas for possession of narcotics and illegal weapons trafficking. He received a five-year prison sentence. He spent three years in prison prior to escaping in a violent confrontation with prison authorities and police that left four individuals dead, including a female who had gone to visit her son in prison. Three of the dead were inmates who either tried to assist or escape with Concord and ten other prisoners.

The brazen jailbreak was a strategically designed plan, organized and overseen by El Hummer. After the jail break, Concord fled to the Southern Mexican state of Chiapas, where he oversaw the Plaza in Tuxtla-Gutierrez. Chiapas is the southernmost state in Mexico and borders the Central American country of Guatemala. Concord's move to Chiapas was not a random act, but a calculated move by the Zetas, as they had plans to take over all narcotics activities in Guatemala.

Guatemala served as a principal transit and storage point for ton-quantities of cocaine loads delivered straight from Colombia, Venezuela, Peru and Bolivia. Estimates showed that drug traffickers were staging 400 metric tons of cocaine in Guatemala before distributing it to Mexico and eventually delivering it to meet the insatiable demand in the United States. That is approximately 400,000 kilograms of cocaine, a business generating over $7 billion dollars in yearly revenue (Time Magazine by Jill Replogle, December 12, 2008). The Zetas lusted for that revenue and salivated at the idea of taking over these operations from the Guatemalan traffickers. The Zetas perceived the Guatemalan trafficking organizations as weak, passive and vulnerable. They were confident that they could take over operations in the country. Control of the state of Chiapas was crucial to the Zetas' plans to do so. Concord immediately proved his worth by recruiting a network of corrupt municipal and state police officers to help extort businessmen and protecting cocaine loads brought into the country. He rented safe houses, purchased vehicles, weapons, ammunition and communication devices. Concord made the most of his tenure in Chiapas, elevating his reputation by assassinating two high-ranking police officers and senselessly torturing and burning a highly respectable businessman over a road rage incident. These murders put El Concord in the spotlight. The Government of Mexico placed a reward of $15 million pesos on his head, making him one of the top ten most wanted men in Mexico.

One afternoon in March 2008, the Zetas led by Miguel Trevino and his second in command, Daniel Perez Rojas, aka "El Cachetes," arranged a meeting with Guatemala's most notorious crime boss, Juan Jose Leon-Ardon aka "El Juancho" to discuss details regarding a shipment of cocaine that was stolen by Juancho and his men from the Zetas. Juancho was notorious for stealing loads of cocaine, selling them and keeping all the profits. The Zetas knew about his reputation and knew that he would eventually steal a load—he just couldn't help himself—and they used his greed and self-indulgence to set him up and thrust their plan into action.

The meeting location had been of Juancho's choosing. The Zetas obliged and met with the heavily guarded Juancho, who had no clue that he had just walked into a death trap. Juancho and his men felt secure in their hometown and home country, but they severely underestimated the Zeta's strategic intelligence. Unbeknownst to Juancho or his men, the Zetas quietly and stealthily established a perimeter around the meeting site and waited for Trevino's signal. Trevino drew his weapon and shot Juancho point blank in the face, killing him instantly, before the meeting even reached the exchange of pleasantries. The Zetas immediately jumped into action and converted the serene tranquility that once was life in Guatemala into a flaming, earth shattering war zone. The Zetas firepower was highly superior to that of the Guatemalans, and a deafening barrage of fragmentation grenades shot from Russian grenade launchers pounded the landscape and thrashed their armored vehicles, leaving the occupants trapped in the kill zone with no way out.

Innocent bystanders scattered like ants to avoid the chaos and crossfire. When the smoke cleared, Juancho, his brother and six bodyguards were found dead among the flaming embers. Inside their armored vehicles, two bodyguards were found burned to a crisp, still holding their rifles dutifully in a death grip. Two other victims died of their wounds in a local hospital. In the blink of an eye, the Zetas had triumphantly invaded Guatemala and the lucrative cocaine transport business that came with the territory. It didn't come without a price, though. The Guatemalan National Police arrested "El Cachetes," whom Trevino and the Zetas left behind to run Zeta operations in

Guatemala a month after the shootout, leaving a vacuum in their newly formed territory.

Because Cachetes' knowledge and expertise proved invaluable to the Zetas operations, they drew up plans to break him out of prison. The job fell squarely on the shoulders of Concord, who Trevino specifically chose for the mission. The mission was highly complex and challenging. It was further jeopardized by threatening phone calls from the Zetas to the Guatemalan national police demanding the release of "El Cachetes." These threats only motivated the Guatemalan National Police to enhance security measures around the prison. They established three security perimeters, one of which included the Guatemalan Army and, for good measure, a fully armed tank in front of the prison.

One plot that was uncovered by the Guatemalan National Police was one in which the Zetas were going to use a "Cachetes" look alike to replace him in prison. They even went so far as to send the double to Guatemala and await further instruction, but the plan did not come to fruition, as the Guatemalan National Police were tipped off to the scheme and apprehended the double before any attempt could be made to replace "Cachetes" in jail. Once they uncovered this scheme, they tightened security at the prison, making it virtually impossible to orchestrate a rescue attempt.

Meanwhile, the Zetas were having their own problems closer to home as Canicon, Amarillo, Hummer, and Karis had all been arrested, killed or forced out of town. As a reward for his service and loyalty to Trevino, Concord became the replacement for Hummer and Karis as the Reynosa Plaza Boss, and our team immediately became aware of the new player in town. We were also in a kind of dilemma because we were receiving very credible information from our Special Forces contacts regarding a location for Canicon.

Both potential operations were developing at a feverish pace and we wanted to be ready for whatever opportunity came first, possibly both at the same time, if necessary, using both the GOPES and the Mexican Special Forces. It turned out that our sources had located Concord at a house in Reynosa Tamaulipas in a quiet, upscale neighborhood known as Residencial Las Fuentes. As before, the GOPES covertly entered the United States through Matamoros and spent the night in McAllen before returning to Mexico. The plan was actually for the GOPES to conduct a quick recon mission on the house and analyze the best plan of attack. Luck favored us that day, because as soon as the GOPES showed up to begin recon, they spotted Concord coming out of the house and entering a black Ford King Ranch pickup truck. The GOPES scrambled to follow and set up a roadblock near the entrance to the neighborhood. Concord had nowhere to go, but this did not deter him from making a mostly futile attempt to escape. The GOPES promptly captured him and returned him to the house, where they seized an AK-47. Fearing a rescue attempt similar to the magnitude of the Zetas' operation for Hummer, the GOPES promptly transported him to the airport and flew him out to Mexico City. Not a single shot was fired and El Concord reached Mexico City before the Zetas even realized he had been taken away.

March 14, 2009: Phase I, complete.

Despite our excitement over the arrest of Concord, there was still a significant amount of work that needed to be completed. Our attention swiftly shifted to the Canicon operation, and we began strategizing our next moves. It has been my experience that when traffickers feel safe, they tend to make mistakes that eventually have a severe impact on their lives. A single mistake in the Zeta organization could cause losing a significant amount of drugs or cash, and that was a dangerous situation for one's well-being.

The Zeta organization sent El Canicon to Saltillo Coahuila to cool off after all the devastation he caused in Monterrey. He had not only terrorized the citizens of Monterrey, but he had brought an unusual amount of heat on the Zetas. Lazcano was angry and wanted to eliminate him, but surprisingly, Miguel Trevino intervened on his behalf and prevented him from receiving a slow torturous death. His instructions were to lie low in a sort of exile until further notice, which he did, initially. But as I said before, one small mistake could cause the house of cards to fall and Canicon made another serious and stupid mistake. Canicon had rented a house in an affluent section of Saltillo, but rather than keep a low profile and fly under the radar, he organized loud parties with armed individuals standing watch. He had cars coming in and out of the house at all hours of the night. Not surprisingly, his new neighbors complained, and one of them, God bless his heart, complained to the Mexican military.

After following up on the complaint and conducting thorough surveillance and taking pictures, military intelligence officers confirmed that the person living at 350 Paseo de Las Rosas, Residencial San Patricio, Saltillo Coahuila, was Sigifredo Nájera Talamantes aka "El Canicon". It was a tremendous stroke of luck—better to be lucky than good.

We were all eager to conduct an operation immediately, but we wanted to make sure we got him this time. So, on March 20, 2009, military intelligence units set up surveillance to confirm Canicon's presence in the house. More than two hundred soldiers from Saltillo and Monterrey were waiting for the signal to begin the operation. At approximately 11 am, El Canicon, still under the effects of a night of serious drinking, arrived at the residence. They made the call and put the plan into action.

At approximately 12 noon, our friends from the Special Forces Unit made entry into the house and captured a surprised and half-drunk Canicon along with six other members of Canicon's entourage, including the regional accountant. The accountant, identified as Yaneth Deyanira Garcia, had in her possession over 10 million pesos, the equivalent of 1.5 million US dollars. Also seized were 8 AK-47s, 3handguns, 24grenades, 4bulletproof vests, 5 vehicles, two of which were fully armored. The potential for a lethal gunfight existed but fortunately, never took place.

We had finally caught the monster who had injected the entire state of Nuevo Leon with fear and terror. They immediately took him to the military base in Saltillo, where they loaded him and his cohorts onto a plane and flew them out to Mexico City.

Canicon's capture made big news throughout Mexico and the United States. In Mexico, President Felipe Calderon congratulated the military on the capture and stated that it was an example of why the military needed to fight the Cartels. We were beyond ecstatic. We had finally brought justice to the memory of the soldiers he mercilessly tortured and killed, as well as to the memory of our friend PFP Comandante Salinas and his partner, also killed by Canicon and Trevino. He was pure evil and had no remorse whatsoever. In spite of his evil nature, our friends in the Special Forces told us that Canicon cried like a baby after his arrest—so much for the big bad tough guy, who would never see freedom again.

March 20, 2009: Phase 2 complete.

El Canicon presented to the media by SEDENA after his capture.
(Photo courtesy of Grupo Reforma / El Norte)

We were running on adrenaline after both captures, but we did not want to relax until we completed the third and final phase of our mission. Our Special Forces team had developed actionable intelligence on an individual named Hector Huerta, who was the Plaza Boss in San Pedro for the Arturo Beltran Leyva Organization, known in DEA circles as the ABLO. The ABLO has its roots in Sinaloa, where at one time they worked hand in hand with Joaquin "El Chapo" Guzman. Arturo Beltran Leyva learned the ropes of the drug trade from Amado Carillo Fuentes, known as "El Senor de los Cielos," in English, "The Lord of the Skies," and worked his way up the totem pole from being an assassin for Amado Carrillo to having his own trafficking cell that worked out of Sonora and Chihuahua.

In the mid to late eighties, Beltran Leyva moved his base of operations to Monterrey Nuevo Leon, a strategic move designed to take advantage of the proximity to the US border crossings at Nuevo

Laredo and Reynosa Tamaulipas. Eventually, Arturo Beltran moved to Acapulco Guerrero but did not give up his strategic holdings in Monterrey. In recent years, the ABLO had developed a conflict with Chapo Guzman as Arturo suspected El Chapo and his people of betraying Arturo's brother, Alfredo and giving information that led to his arrest. As a result, Arturo made an alliance with the Zetas to help fight the Sinaloa cartel in Nuevo Laredo. Hector Huerta was the key figure in the Zetas relationship with Arturo Beltran, and the Zetas let the ABLO operate in Monterrey without reprisals or repercussions.

They designed the move to Guerrero so that the ABLO could receive ton shipments of Colombian cocaine in the port of Guerrero and utilize his assets in Monterrey to store and eventually distribute the cocaine loads to the United States. In leaving Monterrey, Arturo Beltran left Hector Huerta, aka "La Burra", as his chief of operations, or Plaza Boss.

The intelligence we had developed showed that Huerta had a network of corrupt policemen that protected him in San Pedro Garza Garcia Nuevo Leon and carried out assassinations and intelligence collection missions on behalf of the ABLO. San Pedro Garza Garcia was where all US Consulate employees lived and it was unnerving to know that someone so powerful existed amongst us. I found out through an interview of some of Huerta's people that when I first arrived in Monterrey, Huerta knew what hotel I was staying in, what floor I was on and which room I was in—that was how good his intelligence network was. Hector Huerta was also the primary suspect in the assassination of Marcelo Garza y Garza, the Chief of Intelligence for the State of Nuevo Leon, who was killed outside his church while he was talking on his cell phone on September 5, 2006.

Marcelo was a good friend to DEA and his loss stung my colleagues, who had worked closely with him. I never got to meet Marcelo, but his legacy lived on in the hearts of those who were fortunate enough to have known him. He was one of the first high-profile assassinations of a public figure in Monterrey in many years. Similar to El Concord, Huerta was also on Mexico's most wanted list, and authorities offered a reward of 15 million pesos (2 million US dollars) for his capture. We were just as eager to apprehend Huerta as we were in apprehending "El Canicon." The intelligence our friends collected indicated that Huerta was operating freely in downtown San Pedro using an exotic used car lot as his base of operations.

On March 24, 2009, phase three of our operation unfolded.

Military intelligence sent two of their officers in an undercover capacity to the lot to inquire about prices on certain vehicles, hoping to glimpse Huerta or develop some other bits of intelligence. Meanwhile, a team of over eighty soldiers awaited in several vehicles in different parts of San Pedro, waiting for the signal to execute the operation. After being on the premises for about an hour, an armored gray suburban pulled into the lot and Huerta and his bodyguards emerged from the vehicle and walked into the office of the car lot.

The team of soldiers received the signal and converged on the lot, taking Huerta into custody without incident. The arrest triggered other operations around the city of San Pedro, and I received a frantic phone call from my wife informing me that soldiers had surrounded a house situated directly behind ours. It turned out that the house belonged to one of Huerta's girlfriends from where the soldiers seized numerous grenades and a grenade launcher, 3 AK-47s, an AR-15, and a gold-plated handgun. I was astounded to discover that Huerta had a safe house just walking distance from my own—I'm sure it wasn't a coincidence.

Like the other detainees, they took Huerta and four of his cohorts to the military base in Monterrey, loaded them up into a Boeing 727, and flew them out to Mexico City.

March 24, 2008; Phase 3 complete.

It had been an incredible ten days, from the day of the arrest of "El Concord," to the arrests of Huerta and Canicon. The combined efforts of GOPES, SEDENA, and DEA successfully apprehended three highly dangerous cartel leaders, all without firing a single shot. As if that weren't an accomplishment in itself, in another part of the country, our colleagues in Mexico City arrested Vicente Zambada, the son of Ismael "El Mayo" Zambada, the patriarch of the Sinaloa cartel who had largely taken over the operational side of the business for his father.

Those ten days changed the game in the war against the Cartels in Mexico. The arrests made by our counterparts in Northeastern Mexico dealt a significant blow to the leadership structure of both the Zetas and the ABLO. Because of our efforts, we had exacted justice on the murderers of our friends and counterparts. Although nothing we could do would bring them back, we felt satisfaction in knowing the responsible parties were going to pay the price.

After the arrests of Canicon and Huerta, I felt as though someone had lifted a huge load off my shoulders. We would no longer need the San Pedro Police department to keep watch over our house 24 hours a day—frankly, I was not sure I wanted it, after learning the extent of Huerta's intelligence network. It was a tremendous sense of accomplishment for our team, although we still had a mission to accomplish, to capture Z-40, Miguel Trevino and Heriberto Lazcano, "El Lazca."

We would enjoy this victory now, but we still had a big fight ahead of us.

Canicon faced indictment in Washington DC for his involvement in the attack on the US Consulate. Efforts were underway to extradite him to the United States, where he would face trial for the heinous attacks. But bureaucracy is our biggest enemy and time wore on and no extradition took place. They incarcerated him in El Altiplano prison, a maximum-security prison in Mexico City, where Joaquin "El Chapo" Guzman eventually ended up after being on the run for almost fifteen years. El Canicon ended up being Chapo's cell neighbor until "El Chapo" made another outlandish escape and went on the run again. Mysteriously, shortly after Chapo escaped from "El Altiplano," through an elaborately constructed underground tunnel, El Canicon passed away in prison, from what prison officials deem was heart failure, at 35.

I hope that the souls of the people he ruthlessly tortured and killed during his reign of terror haunt and torment him in the afterlife, and it is my sincere opinion that this world is a better place without "El Canicon."

Chapter 9: Another Trifecta

The month of March was extremely successful, but April was now upon us and we wanted to keep striking. The GOPES seemed to be unstoppable. Their well-planned and aggressive style of operations left the Cartels with no solution. On top of that, the GOPES comprised highly trained individuals, and while the original Zetas were former Special Forces soldiers with extensive training, not all Zeta members had that background or possessed special skills. Non-military members who joined the group were required to attend a physically and mentally demanding training regime before being sent out on the street to operate. Most of the time, during operations that resulted in shootouts, the GOPES were going up against adversaries with minimal training, which bent the odds in favor of the GOPES.

We believed we could cripple the Zetas even further if we attacked some of their training camps and apprehended the trainers, along with whoever else was around. In that regard, we had received information regarding a possible training camp in Fresnillo, Zacatecas led by Zeta member Israel Nava-Cortez, aka "El Ostión", or "The Oyster" (I really don't know how these guys come up with some of these nicknames; some are downright comical). El Ostión, like most Zeta Plaza Bosses, had a reputation for violence. El Ostión claimed to have been a former member of Los Kaibiles, the nickname for

Guatemalan Special Forces, and when he initially joined the Zetas, they selected him as Miguel Trevino's chief bodyguard. Eventually, he climbed the ranks, and the Zetas awarded him the Plaza in Guerrero and Oaxaca. The plaza in Guerrero included the lucrative tourist c ity of Acapulco.

The unsuspecting citizens of Acapulco had absolutely no idea of the terror that infiltrated their otherwise serene coastal town. In February 2007, authorities identified him as the person who led an assault on the police station in Acapulco, Guerrero. The assault, carried out with grenade launchers and other high-powered weapons, resulted in the deaths of seven people, including four policemen and three secretaries. As the Plaza Boss in that region, he was also responsible for the collection of extortion payments from nightclubs, restaurants, casinos and other thriving businesses in this tourist town. El Ostión used the same method of operation that Canicon had used in Monterrey. As a result, the once thriving tourist city of Acapulco, playground for Hollywood stars and famous for its beautiful beaches and daredevil cliff divers, fell under the siege of the Zetas and their terror-based campaign. To add to the problem, the Zetas were not the only cartel operating in Acapulco, as Chapo Guzman and his Sinaloa Cartel had a powerful presence in the area, as did Zeta ally, Arturo Belt rán Leyva.

Arturo Beltrán Leyva recognized the importance of the port of Acapulco in receiving multi-ton shipments of cocaine from Colombia, and he had moved his base of operations from Monterrey to Acapulco. He welcomed the Zetas in helping him to eliminate his chief rival, Chapo Guzman, from the area. As a result, the once bustling tourist town became a battlefield between the Zetas and the Sinaloa Cartel, sending the city spiraling into the clutches of fear and despair. The relaxing sound of the waves from the Pacific Ocean pounding the shoreline gave way to gunfire and grenade explosions at all hours of the day and night.

The gunfire wasn't the worst of it. Two police officers were beheaded, and their heads placed outside a municipal building as a message to the police. On another occasion, a head was found floating in the waters of a popular beach resort, and dismembered bodies were randomly deposited in different areas of the city. Shootouts in the streets between the two factions became more and more commonplace and it was all overseen by El Ostión. As in Monterrey, fear, despair and insecurity gripped the citizens of Acapulco; they were afraid to leave their homes and risk being kidnapped or caught in the crossfire between the two cartels.

Tourism declined significantly and businesses closed because of the dangerous climate generated by the Zetas. The Zeta leaders viewed El Ostión as having accomplished his mission in Guerrero, and they had bigger plans for him. They chose him to lead the Plazas in Zacatecas and Aguascalientes, Mexico.

Our information showed that El Ostión was establishing a training camp for Zeta recruits in Fresnillo, Zacatecas, a small mining and agricultural city of over 100,000 inhabitants. Zacatecas is a strategically important state because it borders six other states: Coahuila to the North; San Luis Potosi to the east; Jalisco and Aguascalientes to the south, and Nayarit and Durango to the west. Establishing a training camp in Zacatecas made perfect sense because, once the new recruits completed their training, they could easily dispatch them to any of the six surrounding states immediately. Specifically, they could be sent to Durango, where the Zetas were waging an all-out war on Chapo Guzman and the Sinaloa cartel.

Chapo Guzman and the Sinaloa cartel traditionally oversaw Durango, but the Zetas were greedy, ambitious and, above all, fearless. They wanted control of Durango and its lush region, where marijuana plantations and poppy fields flourished in abundance. So, the training camp was crucial to their plans and to their success in overtaking Durango. Our information indicated El Ostión was living in a house in a well-populated area of Fresnillo and that he had lookouts throughout the city whose job was to inform El Ostión of any military presence in the city. He was not worried about the local police because they were all on his payroll, even acting as additional lookouts for him.

As was commonplace in preparing for high-level operations such as the one we were planning for El Ostión, our biggest challenge was a covert insertion of the GOPES team. Prior operations had succeeded because the target's proximity to the border allowed us to use the United States border cities of McAllen and Brownsville as staging areas prior to insertion into Mexico by the GOPES team to execute the operation. Here, the Zetas vigilant lookout team provided extremely strong protection to Fresnillo, Zacatecas, which is an extremely small and centrally located city. During my time in Mexico, I came to respect the creative ingenuity of the Mexican mindset towards problem solving, and this case highlights that ingenuity.

The GOPES leader came up with the idea to charter a bus to travel from Monterrey to Fresnillo, Zacatecas, under the guise of attending a private convention in the city. The plan was to leave Monterrey and arrive in Fresnillo before daybreak, assuming that all Zeta lookouts would most likely be asleep. If not, they would never suspect that a greyhound bus was packed with a highly trained team ready to eliminate their leader.

On April 8, 2009, the plan was put into action and the GOPES dressed in civilian attire left Monterrey in the chartered bus with a totally unsuspecting civilian bus driver. Meanwhile, another team of GOPES and Mexican Army personnel staged in Zacatecas, Zacatecas, the state capitol, approximately a 45-minute drive to Fresnillo, Zacatecas to reinforce the assault team. They also deployed two helicopters to provide aerial assistance and had a 727 Boeing ready to transport prisoners to Mexico City if needed. At approximately 3:00 am the GOPES leader instructed the bus driver to pull over and the team immediately suited up in their official raid gear, tactical helmets, bullet-proof vests, tactical belts with flash bangs, fragmentation grenades, extra magazine clips, tactical knives and flashlights ready to do battle with the enemy. The team members constantly reassured the terrified bus driver everything would be alright and they would accompany and protect him. After suiting up and getting ready, the team proceeded into Fresnillo, prepared to take on whatever challenges the highly trained Kaibil, had to offer.

The team expected the worst and were ready for it. At approximately 4:30 am, our GOPES team entered Fresnillo under the light of a full moon, undetected, their presence unannounced except for the barking of neighborhood street dogs, but nothing else. As they methodically made their way closer to Ostión's residence, an early rising lookout spotted them, opened fire on them, and alerted Ostión and the rest of his cohorts.

All hell broke loose after that, as Ostión's people fought furiously trying to escape. The GOPES resorted to jumping on rooftops of Ostión's neighbors' houses to get a tactical advantage on him as gunfire and chaos erupted in the sleepy little town. It was intense urban warfare as both the GOPES and Zetas launched grenades at each other. The gunfight lasted well over an hour, with over a thousand rounds being fired before the sun rose in the early morning, in the terrorized sleepy city of Fresnillo.

In the end, Ostión and two of his bodyguards met their demise, and law enforcement officials arrested two others inside the house. Ostión had suffered a fatal gunshot wound that penetrated his skull through his right eye. Nine GOPES personnel were wounded by a fragmentation grenade thrown at the team by Ostión and his now dead companions. Fortunately, the wounds sustained by the GOPES were not life threatening, but it was the first time they had suffered injuries in any of our planned operations. Ostión was eliminated on this operation, but the downside was that we never found the training camp. We were still happy that our team had taken out a valuable member of the Zeta structure; one who would be hard to replace—one who would never train another Zeta recruit ever again or terrorize anyone ever again. Perhaps, the most satisfying result of the operation was that it led to more speculation by the Zeta leadership where the information fueling our operations was coming from. They were questioning, mistrusting, and doubting themselves. Our actions were causing chaos and unrest among their members. They were furious and wanted answers. We had successfully thrown a wrench into their plans in Zacatecas, and their unease and speculation about our next move brought us great satisfaction.

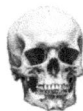

In December 2008, an incident occurred in the neighboring state of Coahuila that shook the entire US community in Mexico and enraged our US Law Enforcement Team. On December 10, 2008, an American citizen, Felix Battista, employed as a security consultant specializing in kidnapping cases and negotiations, was himself kidnapped in the state capital of Saltillo.

The Zetas had overrun the State of Coahuila, like many states and cities all over Mexico. The difference in Coahuila was that the vortex of corruption that existed at all levels within the Coahuila state government empowered the Zetas. From my perspective, the Coahuila State Government was under the control of the Zetas, with Governor Humberto Moreira and other elected officials serving as mere puppets. When Battista was kidnapped, the Coahuila State government had no information about the kidnapper's identity or the reasons behind the abduction. They seemed apathetic, showing no concern whatsoever. The Attorney General of Coahuila didn't even classify it as a kidnapping; he viewed it as a case of a missing person instead.

Mr. Battista was invited to Coahuila to give a presentation to business executives, sharing his expertise on kidnap evasion techniques and providing guidance on how to handle being a kidnap victim. He also provided a separate presentation to members of the Coahuila state police. On the evening of December 10, Battista was at a local restaurant having dinner with some friends when he received a phone call. Battista was negotiating with some kidnappers who had kidnapped his friend Pilar Valdez earlier that same morning, and he had received numerous calls regarding the kidnapping during the dinner. At one point, he got up, left his other phone, laptop and credit card on the table and told his friends to call a certain number if he did not come back. He was last seen entering a vehicle occupied by four males and was not heard from again.

Pilar Valdez was released an hour later.

Days went by and those days turned into weeks and the Coahuila state police Attorney General Jesus Torres Charles had no answers, despite pleas from the United States Consul General for action. Ostensibly, the reason for the lack of interest by the Attorney General was that, according to Mexican Law, if no one makes a demand for ransom, authorities cannot classify the case as a kidnapping. The US team inquired about the possibility of the Mexican Federal Government taking over the case, and authorities informed them that Battista's family needed to file a report. But Battista's wife filed a complaint at the Mexican Consulate in Miami, and they assured her that they would forward the complaint to the appropriate personnel.

On January 9, 2009, during the meeting between the Consul general and Coahuila state officials, it was revealed that the report had not been forwarded to the appropriate federal authorities. This delay was attributed to most personnel being on Christmas vacation. Looks like they really weren't concerned about Battista's well-being. We were getting the same cold shoulder that our agents in Guadalajara, Jalisco, received when Agent Enrique Camarena was kidnapped, tortured, and murdered. Despite our frustration, we had to maintain composure during the meeting to ensure cooperation from the Coahuila authorities. Governor Moreira made a showy pledge to ensure that the case received priority and instructed Attorney General Torres Charles to fully cooperate with the FBI. Attorney General Torres Charles later provided our FBI Attaché with Battista's laptop, thumb drives, and notes. Unbeknownst to the Attorney General, our FBI attaché, on his own initiative, had already interviewed many witnesses who were with Battista at the dinner—witnesses that Coahuila authorities would not have made available otherwise.

At the DEA, we made it a priority to urge our informants to uncover any and all details, regardless of how improbable they may have seemed. In addition, our border offices diligently instructed their informants to gather all details pertaining to the Battista case. Unfortunately, as with thousands of similar cases in Mexico, the case went cold. The lack of clues and lack of interest by the Coahuila State Police dumbfounded us. But we continued our investigation anyway, and little by little started picking up pieces of information from our sources. The primary piece of information we derived was the identity of the Plaza Boss for Saltillo, German Torres Jimenez, aka "Z-25," aka "El Tatanka."

El Tatanka, an original Zeta, was a former Special Forces member who had deserted his unit. He was recruited by Heriberto Lazcano for his exceptional skills in tactics, logistics, and kidnapping. Originally, they assigned him to the Veracruz plaza, a bustling training ground where he instructed new recruits in tactics and firearms handling. It is believed that the Zetas had over four training camps in the state of Vera Cruz. After serving well in Veracruz, he was reassigned to the Mexican border town of Comales, Tamaulipas which is south of Starr County, Texas, a gateway for the flow of narcotics into the United States and home to high-level drug traffickers associated with the Gulf Cartel and Zetas. While in Comales, El Tatanka oversaw the organization and movement of massive shipments of cocaine into the United States, specifically through cities like Rio Grande City, Roma, and Garciasville, Texas. After serving well in this capacity, he was promoted to the level of Plaza Boss for the city of Saltillo, Coahuila.

Saltillo, Coahuila, founded in 1577, is approximately 160 miles south of the Texas border and is a key industrial city with many US Manufacturing firms based in the city and surrounding areas. The city earned the nickname the Detroit of Mexico because of the significance of its automotive industry, with assembly plants of companies like Chrysler, General Motors, Mercedes Benz, and Delphi located there. The population in Saltillo is approximately 825,000 people, making it one of the biggest cities in Mexico. At one time, Saltillo served as the Capitol of Saltillo y Tejas which covered the region of what is now Texas, until the Texas War of Independence and the founding of the independent republic of Texas. One can spend days perusing Saltillo's world-class museums, exploring and admiring the buildings in its historic colonial center, or enjoying the cool climate and take in the breathtaking view of the city perched above the mirador(viewpoint). Restaurants abound serving the favorite local fare cabrito (baby goat), or thick juicy steaks from locally raised livestock served with guacamole and handmade corn or flour tortillas, accompanied by the wine produced from local grape vineyards, or the apple wines produced from local apple orchards; vendors are found throughout the city offering their wares such as silver, leather goods, wool blankets locally produced peaches, apples, grapes and the famous serapes, while the sounds of mariachi and Norteno music waft on the cool breeze coming off the Sierra Madre.

Because of its unique diversity and rich cultural history, Saltillo is one of the most interesting towns in all of Mexico. It was a shame that the Zetas turned this beautiful city into a war zone and terrorized its citizens. Part of what motivated us to pursue the Zetas and their leaders relentlessly was to restore peace to cities like Saltillo, Monterrey, Acapulco, and many other cities throughout Mexico. This would enable local citizens and tourists from all over the world to come and witness first-hand the beauty that Mexico offered. For instance, I always dreamed of taking my children to Saltillo's Museo del Desierto, a museum that displays dinosaur skeletons and ancient fossils. Unfortunately, I never got the chance because of the unsafe atmosphere created by the Zetas.

Tatanka was now the Plaza Boss and our sources told us he was directly responsible for Battista's kidnapping, and that Lazcano and Miguel Trevino were not happy with him for carrying out the kidnapping without their authorization. He was in the unenviable position of being on both the Zetas radar, and ours. Trevino was furious because, once again, the heat of the United States Government was on him because of Tatanka's actions. His plan was to hunt him down and kill him personally. This concerned us because we knew Trevino could find him easily with his vast network of Zetas operating throughout the country and we wanted to find him and keep him alive so we could interview him about the fate of Battista.

The race to track down Tatanka was on between Trevino and our team. Trevino had the advantage because he spread the word amongst the Zetas that anyone in the organization who helped hide Tatanka would also face torture and death. Our team just needed a lucky break, which we received when our source provided us with a phone number Tatanka was using. We got to work immediately and began tracking the phone. Because of the signal intelligence (SIGINT) provided by the phone activity, we determined Tatanka was in Poza Rica Vera Cruz, at a house in a subdivision called Colonia Los Laureles.

We provided the GOPES with the information, and they mobilized a team from Mexico City to Vera Cruz. On April 24, 2009, at approximately 3 am the GOPES cautiously approached the residence, fully aware of Tatanka's tactical abilities but not knowing how many people were inside the residence nor what weapons they had at their disposal. As the GOPES approached the residence, they were met with gunfire. In response, they entered the residence and pounced on a wounded Tatanka and four accomplices. Tatanka suffered non-life-threatening wounds to the buttocks. After providing medical attention and stabilizing him, they immediately whisked all five away from the residence, loaded them up into two helicopters, and flew them out to Mexico City.

The operation was conducted without the knowledge of the local Veracruz authorities because of Tatanka's influence over them from his previous assignment in Veracruz. .After the media presented Tatanka in Mexico City, they took him to a local hospital where he underwent surgery for his wounds. He was now in federal custody, and we were champing at the bit to go interview him. One of our DEA team members and the FBI Legal Attaché flew to Mexico City to interview him, but the results were not what we expected. The anesthesia given to him during his surgery left him disoriented and he complained about pain in his abdomen. He showed a fresh surgical scar on his stomach to our team members and demanded an explanation for why they had opened his abdomen when he had been shot in the buttocks. It was a legitimate question, and one to which we had no answer. Sometimes justice is dealt out in mysterious ways.

Tatanka denied having anything to do with Battista's kidnapping. Our team members described him as brusque, uneducated and unsophisticated, so much so that it was hard to believe that this guy was once a Special Forces soldier and a leader within the Zeta organization. We were happy that we got to him before Trevino, but it was a bitter pill to swallow that we had made no advancements into the Battista investigation, as we wanted to bring some sense of closure to Mr. Battista's family.

In interviews with sources, we learned that Trevino and the Zetas believed that all DEA. FBI, ICE and Consulate personnel had chips with GPS trackers secretly implanted in their bodies in case of a kidnapping incident. So, the theory brought to us was that Battista was killed, and his body then disintegrated in a barrel of acid to destroy the chip and frustrate rescue efforts. Regrettably, no trace of Mr. Battista's body has ever been found, leaving his fate unresolved. Sadly, cases such as these are all too common in Mexico. My prayers are with Mr. Battista's family, and I hope they find peace and solace and know that we made every effort to resolve his disappearance.

As if the logistics of both operations weren't stressful already, Monterrey was also dealing with a widespread outbreak of swine flu. People were dying from this virus, and it caused panic throughout Mexico and the rest of the world. The Consulate was prepared to evacuate personnel in case the epidemic worsened. The situation was aggravated by a scarcity of the antiviral drug Tamiflu, making it even more dire. Schools were closing, businesses were shutting down, flights were being canceled, people were staying home, affecting restaurants and other entertainment venues. Those that did venture out wore sterile surgical masks adding a surreal element to everyday life. People were wearing masks everywhere—at the grocery store, banks, church, even while driving or inside bars! This, coupled with the terror the Zetas were generating, produced a feeling of doom. It felt as though the world was ending.

However, it did not prevent my counterparts in Matamoros from completing the month by delivering another serious blow to the

Gulf cartel. As I mentioned in a previous chapter, El Karis' brother Gregorio Sauceda Gamboa, aka "El Goyo", had once been second in command to Gulf Cartel boss Osiel Cardenas Guillen and enjoyed immense power within the organization and at one time oversaw the Nuevo Laredo, Reynosa and Matamoros Plazas. However, his health declined because of his cocaine addiction and alcoholism. Because of his addiction, he lost his ability to lead and make strong decisions, and ultimately, he was stripped of all power and banished to his hometown of Matamoros.

El Goyo had once been a state judicial policeman and in his prime oversaw the smuggling of between 10 to 30 tons of cocaine per month for the Gulf Cartel and ordered the deaths of many rivals and presumed rivals. When Osiel Cardenas was captured, he temporarily took on the role of the cartel's boss. There was a 30-million-peso reward for his capture and was one of the most wanted men in all of Mexico. Despite this notoriety, he lived peacefully and quietly in Matamoros, Tamaulipas, without being bothered by any law enforcement authority. That all changed when my DEA counterpart in Matamoros uncovered actionable information about him. El Goyo thought he had made it and retired without having to answer for his crimes, but as with all traffickers, no matter how powerful, his time had come and on April 30, 2009, the GOPES, all wearing sterile mouth covers conducted an operation and captured El Goyo at his residence in Matamoros, along with his wife and bodyguard. They also seized an arsenal of weapons that served no purpose for Goyo, as he did not even get off one round of the 4500 rounds seized.

El Goyo was surprised that it happened, but he should have anticipated it after his brother Karis' death, especially considering his stature as one of Mexico's most wanted men. El Goyo, his wife and his bodyguard were all transported to Mexico City wearing sterile mouth covers to protect them from the swine flu. For the second month in a row, in an unprecedented display of teamwork by the GOPES, DEA, FBI and ICE, three major cartel leaders had been captured and taken out of business. Although chaos ruled Mexico during this time frame, we overcame and complete another trifecta.

Chapter 10: Vortex of Corruption

The deep-rooted corruption in Mexico has persisted for centuries—generations of betrayals, bribes, broken promises, and lies have left a trail of shattered dreams, fractured families, lost fortunes, and ruined lives. Every aspect of everyday life in Mexico intertwines with corruption, and people perpetuate it daily, from the guy who greases the palms of the maître' d at a fine restaurant for a table without a reservation, to the cartel member who pays off government officials for special favors. People expect to get their palms greased and everyone knows it, from the rich businessman in the Armani suit to the beggar on the street. So, those who have the means to do so continue enjoying the extra benefits attached to their generosity and those that don't have the means basically get screwed and are left on the outside looking in. For political corruption, it is the public who suffers, forced to witness politicians luxuriating in the benefits of their public service. It is a vicious cycle. In Mexico, the cops on the street struggle to make ends meet, often resorting to extorting the public just to put food on their tables, a practice known as a "mordida" or "a bite." Everyone knows it, but nobody does anything about it. The governors of states don't care, as long as they are receiving their bite. The mayors don't care as long as it doesn't interfere with their bite. So it goes on and on, the general public continually getting screwed as life goes on and the worst part is that everybody hangs their heads down in acceptance.

In Monterrey, the Zetas exploited the situation and offered substantial sums of money to government officials and cops in every municipality. They sought information about potential military operations that could affect their business, potential kidnap victims, rival cartel members, and also requested protection whenever necessary. The Zetas organization's tentacles of corruption were extensive and far-reaching, ensnaring hundreds of officials and infecting the social network like a malignant growth.

Our newly formed relationship with the Army was paying off big dividends in the form of intelligence on the Zetas' local leadership structure. Our intelligence indicated that a Zeta, code named "El Colosio." oversaw the Monterrey suburb of San Nicolas de los Garza, and had most of the police force in his pocket. It made sense why the Zetas ensured the San Nicolas police. After all, with a population of at least five hundred thousand people, San Nicolas stood as the third largest city in Nuevo Leon. It is home to the Universidad Autonoma de Nuevo Leon (UANL) and several major factories, such as Cemex, one of the largest building materials producers in the world; and Vitro, the largest glass manufacturer in Mexico and leaders in the glassmaking industry worldwide; and it is also home to the Tigres, a professional soccer team associated with the UANL and one of the most popular teams in Mexico. It is also home to the Mexican Army's Fourth Region.

The Mexican Army is divided into twelve regions throughout the country, and each region has a zone of responsibility. There are forty-five zones throughout the country. Our team, under the command of the Fourth Region, operated in the seventh zone. The tactical reasons for the Zetas flooding San Nicolas were very clear to us. As the third largest city in Nuevo Leon, San Nicolas had a sizeable police department that was highly underpaid, thus highly susceptible to corruption. With over several hundred police officers at their disposal, the Zetas could easily monitor the coming and going of traffic in and out of the Fourth Region's military base, which included our vehicles, as we were frequent visitors to the Fourth Zone.

Juan Daniel Carranco Salazar, aka "El Colosio" was not an original Zeta nor did he have any military experience. Originally from Nuevo Laredo, he was a welder by trade and at one time worked for the city of Nuevo Laredo as a traffic cop. He left the police department in 2002 and tried to find work as a welder. However, because his vision was failing, jobs were scarce. Bills piled up. His marriage was on the rocks and his mother had a heart condition that required expensive medical treatment that he could not afford. He hit rock bottom when the bank repossessed his house, and his wife left him to care for his ailing mother on his own. It was then that an old friend from the police department recruited him to work for the Zetas. A job which he readily accepted, as it paid $3000 pesos per month, not much, but more than he was making as a welder.

El Colosio started as a lookout (halcon) on the streets of Nuevo Laredo, reporting on any movement by the Army or Federal Police. He climbed up the ranks, working in cities such as Matamoros, Ciudad Guerrero, Reynosa, and Rio Bravo. Eventually, he arrived in Nuevo Leon and received the assignment as the primary bodyguard for the Plaza Boss in Cadereyta, known as "El Animal," who was later killed in Durango, Durango, Mexico. They then assigned him as the primary bodyguard for "El Rambo," the Plaza Boss of San Nicolas.

Eventually, they reassigned El Rambo, and "El Colosio" became the new Plaza Boss for the Zetas in San Nicolas. Little did he know that by accepting the position, he had also gained a large target on his b ack.

As far as the Army was concerned, all Zetas played a role in the deaths of their nine comrades killed by Canicon, especially Zetas who held leadership roles. In the mindset of the Army, all Zetas had knowledge of the orders to kidnap military personnel and turn them over to Canicon—so, every single Zeta was to be held accountable. The intelligence DEA and SEDENA developed on Colosio was highly actionable. We knew he scheduled weekly meetings with members of the police force to distribute payment for their services. Colosio's girlfriend, a member of the San Nicolas police force known to us as Aida aka "La Guera" or "the blonde one", arranged the meetings in secluded and desolate areas of San Nicolas. We had received valuable information that El Colosio was going to have a gathering with some of his most trusted men at a Quinta, a country home, to celebrate El Cinco de Mayo and we were salivating at the prospect of taking him into custody during this assembly.

However, we had to wait for the right moment to ensure his capture, and waiting was something we all loathed. The worst part of any operation is the wait prior to the action. The fear of the unknown intensifies during this wait time. One can actually hear the seconds ticking away with each heartbeat, as time slowly drifts off into infinity, like smoke in the wind. Seconds feel like hours, hours feel like weeks. Everything seems to slow down as eternity slackens to a near complete standstill. To make matters worse, the month of May marked the beginning of summer and extreme heat in Monterrey's climate. Mountains, which seem to trap all the radiant heat in the region and prevent any breeze from providing relief to the parched sunbaked souls living within it, surround the place.

Today was no exception. The brunt of summer bore down on the region with a sizzling and suffocating heat, nearing the hundred degree mark. To counteract the heat and anxiety, the SEDENA team used the wait time to check their weapons, equipment, ammunition supply, first aid kits, tire pressure, oil and fuel levels, again and again. When they were done, they checked their partner's equipment to make double sure everyone was prepared for whatever the Zetas came with. No one spoke a word and a look of calm, controlled determination graced the sweat stained faces of each soldier as they waited for the call. Waiting is an art. One can fly into a senseless rage waiting for the outcome, or one can be calm and patient and think about every scenario methodically. Only the most patient fishermen and hunters are rewarded with the finest catch or game animal, and we hoped to be rewarded for our patience as well, as difficult as waiting was for us. We were patient. We were ready.

We were rewarded for our patience as the call came in just as dusk settled over the city, washing the sky with an eerie mix of orange, pink and violet hues as wild coyotes howled in the distant mountain range. According to the source, Colosio was expected to attend the heavily guarded Cinco de Mayo party at Quinta El Mezquital, potentially with the help of San Nicolas Police units. The source mentioned that there would be an abundance of food, cocaine, marijuana, liquor, beer, and music. They stated that around 11 PM, a parade of prostitutes would be brought to the Quinta. Colosio would select two or maybe three for himself and then depart to an unknown hotel in Monterrey. The source said that Colosio was at the Quinta now and was partying with the others while he waited for the prostitutes.

We delivered the information to the team, who immediately looked up the coordinates to the Quinta and planned the operation while we still had some time on our side. Conveniently enough, the Quinta was in Apodaca, Nuevo Leon, in the same city and relatively close to the Army base, which made things just a little easier for the t eam.

We decided that four trucks, each carrying eight men, would leave the base at staggered intervals in case the Zetas lookouts were watching the base for activity. We did not want to arouse suspicion by sending all four trucks at the same time. Once clear of the base, they received instructions to set up in tactical areas near the Quinta and await the assault team, traveling in a separate truck. It was unlikely that the Zetas would have lookouts set up on a Sunday, on the day of a big party, but we took no chances. We waited as all four trucks departed and reported that they were in position and ready to go.

Our veins pulsed with the familiar rush of adrenaline as the last team reported in, confirming their readiness. I made the sign of the cross and prayed for the safety of the team as we gave them the green light. With the element of surprise on their side, the assault team charged towards the Quinta. As they approached the Quinta, they saw various men, clearly armed, milling around carelessly, supposedly guarding the entrance. Their eyes widened with disbelief and then filled with horror as they saw the assault team charging towards them and their party.

"Guachos!" shouted the primary lookout to the others and immediately opened fire on the approaching team. The others joined him and started opening up on the team as all chaos broke loose!

"Guachos! Corran pendejos saquen al jefe de aqui!"(Soldiers!! Run idiots!! Get the boss out of here!)

A barrage of gunfire riddled the Quinta as people started running in all directions, firing rounds at the team to get away or merely survive. As the team slowly and methodically advanced upon the entrance to the Quinta, gunfire met them from the rear flank. Blue and red lights cutting through the gun smoke like a giant outdoor disco lit the night up as bullets whizzed by the assault team. The lights came from a marked Apodaca police unit occupied by four officers who were now engaged in the gunfight with our team. As the team returned fire, the screeching sound of burning rubber filled the air as the four officers frantically tried to flee in reverse, crashing into a parked trailer. All four got out and ran into the darkness dressed in full uniform. Meanwhile, the gunfight proceeded until the team breached the entrance and the people left in the Quinta gave up.

Colosio, however, was nowhere to be found. He had escaped.

The glaring question was, how? How the hell did this guy get away? There was no time to think about the obvious question or wait for the smoke to clear. There was work to do, so the team conducted a methodical search of every nook and cranny inside the main building, while another part of the team began collecting evidence. The team made six arrests at the scene, with five of the individuals being police officers from the San Nicolas Police Force. The team took all defendants to the military base for processing and interrogation. After all the evidence had been collected, the team seized 24 vehicles, one of which was fully armored; 25 firearms, including AK-47s, AR-15s and 5.7 mm handguns, famously known as "cop killers," 7 grenades, 76 kilos of marijuana, 1 kilo of cocaine, 5 sets of handcuffs, and 1 of the famous tablas. The best evidence seized, though, were several cell phones that were left behind or dropped in the assault's chaos. The interviews of the defendants painted a clearer picture of what took place during the assault. According to one defendant, when the assault took place, a call went out via Nextel radio to Colosio's right-hand man and head of security, El Tiburon, also a San Nicolas policeman. Colosio had been hit and wounded during the attack and had been led out the back of the Quinta by one of the Zetas. They ran for their lives until Tiburon met and rescued them. The information about the escape and Tiburon's involvement encouraged us, and because Tiburon's number came up in many of the seized phones along with several other interesting numbers, including one for Aida, Colosio's police officer girlfriend.

We immediately started tracking Tiburon's phone, hoping to get a clear fix on his location, before he dropped the phone and went into permanent hiding. He had a good head start on us and we were sure he had already fled the area. Initially, our hopes were dashed as we did not receive a signal off his phone, indicating that it was off and he had most likely discarded it. We had nothing left but to strategize our next move. Despite being tired and frustrated, we continued to hope that we would find something of value in the phones that we had seized. Our intelligence indicated Aida, Colosio's girlfriend, to be the liaison between the Zetas and the entire San Nicolas, Apodaca, Escobedo police forces, and she was in charge of making payoffs to them on behalf of the Zetas. We agreed she would be the next logical target, in order to put more pressure on Colosio and to help unwind the enormous knot of corrupt police officials.

As we were discussing our plans for Aida's capture, the military analyst in charge of monitoring the signal off Tiburon's phone interrupted our meeting and breathlessly announced that a signal was being received off Tiburon's phone and it was showing an address in San Nicolas. We were ecstatic, but skeptical. He could have given the phone to someone else or discarded it. Either way, we wanted to be sure it was him before taking any enforcement action. The team sent members of the intelligence unit to conduct surveillance of the house from where the signal was emanating—to solidify our belief that Tiburon was actually there.

Surveillance was difficult to conduct because everyone in the neighborhood knew each other and was familiar with the vehicles each other used. Strange vehicles and strange faces were met with suspicion, and in this and many neighborhoods in Monterrey, word traveled fast whenever a stranger was detected. In order to meet this challenge, we decided a taxi would be used to enter the neighbor- hood, with a driver, and a male and female passenger all part of the team. If they spotted anything that showed Tiburon was at the sus- pected residence, they were to signal a team of twelve soldiers in three separate vehicles, standing by near the residence. Best case scenario, they could drive by the residence at least twice before arousing the suspicions of the residents or neighbors, then all hell would surely bre ak loose.

It was decided that the female member of the team, code name "Lolita," would be dropped off on foot about two houses south of the target house and report her observations to the team. The taxi was to drive north to the end of the street, do a u-turn and pick her up as she walked. It was a much better option than driving by twice and it gave the team more time and a better opportunity to make the correct decision. If she were stopped or questioned, she would use the cover story that she was looking for her aunt's house and was lost. The good thing about the Army is that most recruits were not local and were from other states and other regions of the country, meaning accents and dialects were different, so we felt confident about her cover story. At approximately 11:00 am, the plan was put into action. They dropped off Lolita, backpack and all, at the agreed location. She walked slowly, stopped in front of the target house and got on the phone, pretending to be lost, asking for directions, all while observing the house for clues that Tiburon was inside. The team remained tense, prepared to take immediate action if things got out of hand and if Lolita was threatened. The minimal traffic worked to the team's advantage in case they needed a quick getaway. After what seemed like an hour, Lolita started walking north on the street, briskly this time. The taxi met her as she walked northbound, and she practically jumped into the rear passenger section and said "Ahi esta!" (He is there!) Under the carport of the residence, she had observed a vehicle that was partially covered by a tarp—a San Nicolas PD marked vehicle! She also said that she observed a male subject peek out from the doorway of the residence but could not tell if it was Tiburon. Although she did not positively identify Tiburon, the facts added up: Tiburon's phone was pinging from the house and there was a San Nicolas PD marked vehicle in the driveway. It was time to send in the team.

As the team arrived and approached the front door of the residence, they were met by El Tiburon himself, who had a gun in his hand. He quickly loaded a round into the chamber, but wisely surrendered when he realized he was outnumbered. The team immediately took him into custody without firing a shot, which was a major accomplishment, especially considering the team found an AR-15 loaded and ready to go, along with a Colt .223 and a Berretta 9mm handgun, 5 cellphones, 3 two-way radios and numerous baggies of marijuana ready for street distribution.

The real work had just begun as we were eager to see if Tiburon would give up Colosio's location. In his confession Tiburon admitted to rescuing Colosio, taking him to a rendezvous point in downtown Monterrey and handing him off to another Zeta, Plaza Boss, also nicknamed Tiburon, who was in charge of the Santiago Plaza, just outside Monterrey. He said he did not know where they took Colosio afterwards. He said that he was in charge of all lookouts monitoring the activities of the Army at the Fourth region base and the Seventh Zone base. Tiburon remained defiant and vowed that the Zetas would retaliate for the actions taken on Colosio and himself. Pretty bold talk for a guy in the custody of the soldiers he just shot at a few days ago and whose movements he reported to his Zeta buddies—either that, or just plain dumb!

One thing the team extracted from Tiburon was the true name of Colosio's girlfriend, a person whom we knew about but had no clue as to her true identity. Aurora Aida Villarreal, aka "La Guera", an active San Nicolas Police official and liaison between the Zetas and corrupt police officials from various police departments. We also found phone numbers for Plaza Bosses Tiburon 2 and Rambo, but our priority was La Guera. The big gun of the Mexican Army and DEA was now pointed at her, and she had no clue!

Tracking La Guera would not be difficult, being that she had a set work schedule, even though she dumped her phone after the Colosio operation. A quick analysis of her old phone revealed some frequently called numbers we explored as well, and we identified her new phone number within ten days. Once we had her number, we started analyzing it to determine what we call a pattern of life. Most humans are creatures of habit. The most predictable pattern in most of our lives is our sleep routine. Most times, we can determine where a person lives, frequents or stays at because usually the phone's signal will remain in a particular area for an extended period, which leads to the conclusion that the target is sleeping at a specific location. Once we determine a good pattern of life, we plan the operation.

In Aida's case, we decided that the best time to apprehend her was while she was on duty. As I mentioned before, she had absolutely no idea that she was now a target. Sources told us she acted as though nothing had happened. She thought she was untouchable because of her badge and protected by the brotherhood of corrupt cops and her allegiance to the Zetas. Sometimes, a sense of invincibility on the target's part worked to an advantage for us, and we were ready to jump on it.

On Monday, June 8, 2009, as she was getting ready to start her shift, a team of ten soldiers in two separate vehicles went to the vicinity of the San Nicolas Police station and found her as she was getting out of her white Jeep Cherokee. She saw them and immediately ran away in a panic, but was no match for the team of soldiers. There was nowhere to run or nowhere to hide anymore. The look of terror and disbelief belied her senses, but she still had the state of mind to send out a distress call via her Nextel, after which an uncanny look of calm and assuredness took over her expressions of shock and fear. Then all hell broke loose. There was no way of predicting the wave of chaos that unfolded after Aida's arrest.

The arrest appeared to have taken place quietly and without incident, but then the stillness of an otherwise quiet evening was shattered by a lone siren wailing in the distance. Then another siren joined in, followed by more, until it seemed as though a monstrous symphony of deafening police sirens had overtaken the entire city Traffic started backing up as automatic gunfire, screeching tires, and incessant honking horns filled the air in the distance. The Zetas had responded to Aida's distress call, and they came with all they had—including the corrupt cops on their payroll—to rescue her. Police units from almost every city in the Monterrey suburbs came to her aid, including Guadalupe PD, Escobedo PD, San Nicolas PD, and Apodaca PD. More than 100 armed and uniformed police officials came to her rescue as the Zetas began systematically blocking all the main roads throughout the city. They set fires, hijacking buses, tractor trailers and vehicles at gunpoint to grind traffic to a standstill, leaving civilians horrified, anxious and helpless. Amid the sounds of distant gunfire, relentlessly honking horns, State Police helicopters angrily flying overhead, the smell of smoke from tires burning in the street and the shouting of the local cops demanding Aida's release, she was nowhere to be found. Luckily for us, the team had whisked Aida out to the military base before the fun started, rendering the chaotic rescue attempt useless. The chaos was so surreal that it felt like a nightmare, and just when one thought the situation couldn't possibly deteriorate further, it did.

The Federal and State police arrived on the scene to disperse the angry nest of over 100 protesting police officers, confident that they would listen to reason, pack up and move on. Instead, they experienced fierce resistance, as if throwing gasoline on a raging fire. It was an intense standoff of huge proportions, over 150 heavily armed Federal Police versus 100 local cops. Local cops threatened the Feds and pointed their long weapons at them, fingers on the trigger, ready to shoot, daring them to act. In response, the Feds drew their weapons and pointed at them as well, ready to respond if one were to get shot.

It is truly remarkable that, in such a highly tense and dangerous situation, not a single police officer discharged their weapon. The intense standoff and Zeta blockades dragged on for over three long hours, culminating in the apprehension of eleven local police officers from San Nicolas and Escobedo who were involved in the confrontation. Despite the chaos, not a single police chief arrived at the scene to organize their respective teams and restore order. Furthermore, no chief took the time to clarify why their troops had ventured so far from their assigned jurisdictions.

The answer is all too obvious.

This particular incident led to the nickname "polizetas," a term used to describe corrupt police officers working for the Zeta cartel. At the end of the day, the team successfully achieved their goal of apprehending Aida. To their surprise, they also discovered a treasure trove of intelligence from the eleven (11) phones found in her truck. Among the findings was a detailed list of corrupt cops on the Zeta payroll, complete with specific amounts paid to each individual. There were hundreds of cops on the list, including chiefs of police and other high-ranking officers of different police departments. Because of this discovery, the Army conducted a thorough investigation which ultimately resulted in the apprehension of 74 state and municipal law enforcement officials across the state, all of whom were found to have been aiding the Zetas. It was mind-boggling, but little did we know, there was so much more waiting to be discovered.

Chapter 11: Follow the Money - The Hunt for "El Rambo"

"Follow the money!" Our former administrator, a former AUSA who ruled the DEA with an iron fist pounded into our heads this phrase. She struck fear in the hearts of hardened DEA agents in Headquarters Senior Management positions in Washington, DC and took pleasure in belittling them at every turn. The result was a knee jerk reaction; the philosophy of follow the money soon replaced the philosophy of go undercover and seize the dope. This new mission statement was constantly repeated to agents doing the grunt work in the field. For all the shortcomings in her character, and all the horror stories we heard about her in the field, I agreed with the philosophy.

Criminal organizations thrive on money, and when their source of money is cut off, it weakens and infuriates them. And when they are pissed off, they tend to make irrational decisions, eventually leading to their downfall. Our administrator eventually retired, but the philosophy lives on to this day. It was with this philosophy in mind that we started planning our next step. We had a ton of intelligence to work with from Aida's phones, and the narco-payroll list. The amounts paid to all the corrupt officials were staggering, totaling over 5 million pesos ($450,000 USD) a month. After Colosio evaded our attempt to arrest him, they transferred him to Cancun, where the Army eventually apprehended him in that state. The captures of Aida, Colosio and Tiburon, accompanied by the arrests of the 7 4 police officials, created a large vacuum within the Zeta leadership in Monterrey. Cops were not getting paid their bi-weekly stipend from the Zetas because of their absence. We had seized none of their monies, but we took out the key people who paid them—and it hurt them. Some cops stopped showing up for work altogether.

It took us awhile to piece together the intelligence we had seized, but we soon learned that there were two Zetas now taking charge of Colosio's role, but on a much higher level, in charge of paying not only the local cops, but cops throughout the entire state of Nuevo Leon. They were code named Rambo and Tiburon 2. Real bad asses. Not only in charge of payoffs, but also for kidnappings and extortions throughout the region. Rambo had been on Z-40, Miguel Trevino's personal security detail and was rewarded with the Plaza of San Nicolas to replace Colosio. Tiburon 2 oversaw the citric region of Nuevo Leon, comprised by the cities of Santiago, Allende, Linares, General Teran, Montemorelos and Hualahuises (pronounced Wallaweeses).

The climate in this Nuevo Leon region is conducive to the cultivation of citrus orchards, comprising oranges, grapefruits, lemons, limes and tangerines that flourish in the ideal climate of the area. There is only one word to describe this enchanting region of the state, tranquility. The breathtaking views of the countryside, nestled within the Sierra Madre Occidental, invoke peacefulness, one with nature and tranquility. A drive through the region in the springtime, among the backdrop of the sun kissed mountainside, will reward one with the dazzling aroma of citrus blossoms wafting through the air, that attracts thousands of exotic butterflies and honeybees. The citrus industry coexists with the production of honey, as bees are attracted to the citrus blossoms for their nectar. The bees produce honey, making the region—specifically Allende—the largest producer of honey in Mexico.

The region is home to the Rio Ramos and several creeks and streams where visitors come to camp, hike and enjoy the magnificent sunsets that reflect off the mountains, bidding all a goodnight as the day fades away into swirling colors of orange, pink, purple and blue, giving way to the fluorescent moonlight surrounded by a backdrop of zillions of stars. It is this lure of tranquility that enticed many wealthy families in Nuevo Leon and surrounding states to purchase tracts of land and build large ranch houses, referred to in Mexico as Quintas, which served as a respite or get away from the fast-paced city life and allow one to enjoy nature and the culinary delights native to Nuevo Leon.

There is nothing better than the smell of roasted cabrito (kid goat), borrego (lamb) or plain old carne asada, (grilled beef) on a moonlit, star-studded night with a cold beer in your hand surrounded by friends and family. In the mornings, there is no better way to start your day than with a satisfying breakfast of machacado con huevo. The spicy salsa, refried beans, fresh white cheese, and handmade flour tortillas complete the mouthwatering meal, which is best enjoyed with a steaming cup of café de olla. After breakfast, most families go to the Presa de la Boca (la Boca dam) in Santiago, designated as a Pueblo Magico (Magic City), for jet skiing, canoeing or just camping out on the lakeside. Another option would be to visit the renowned Cola de Caballo (Horsetail waterfall), a popular tourist spot in Mexico. Here, visitors can indulge in nature walks, horse riding, or even try their hand at bungee jumping. After partaking of either one of these activities, the day would not be complete without a visit to

Oscar's Drinks in Santiago, where the bartenders prepare the best Micheladas in the world and a wide variety of other drinks. Besides the drinks, the best thing about Oscar's is watching the bartenders, who must be magicians, prepare one's drink. It is comparable to watching a highly skilled Japanese chef performing and preparing your food right before you. This was Quinta life. Tranquil, peaceful family-oriented fun, until Tiburon 2 and the Zetas arrived and discovered a gold mine, a target rich environment for kidnappings and ex tortion.

Many owners of citrus groves were quite successful and had amassed a decent amount of wealth, land and farm equipment, making them and their family members ideal targets for kidnappings and extortion; And the wealthy Quinta owners? Tiburon 2 and the Zetas salivated at the prospect of kidnapping one of them or a member of his family or even a trusted employee. Anyone who had any close relation to someone who appeared to be wealthy was a target, even the maids, cooks, gardeners, and nannies. Nobody was safe. Fear overcame the region as Tiburon 2 and his team followed the Zeta operations model and extorted business owners, restaurants, property owners and even street vendors. Cops on their payroll, performe d traffic stops on people driving in luxury vehicles or newer looking vehicles and turned them over to Tiburon 2 for possible extortion or kidnapping. It was a target rich environment for the kidnapping trade. This web ensnared many "juniors" (children of wealthy parents), forcing their parents to pay a steep price, while others simply vanished without a trace.

Just as El Canicon did with Barrio Antiguo, Tiburon ruined the economy of the region and the lives of many families. Businesses closed down, tourism declined, and the Zetas forced many farm and

Quinta owners to sign over their properties, leaving behind every-thing of value such as farm equipment, livestock, horses, cars, trucks, jet skis, four wheelers, motorcycles, and boats. However, this pales in comparison to the pain this caused many families of kidnap victims that survived, and the even more immense pain of those that did not survive. The worse part of all this? Nobody in the Mexican Govern-ment took any action or showed concern, except for SEDENA and our team. If the Mexican Government did care, it seemed they took no action to solve it.

In the aftermath of the operation on Colosio, Rambo was laying low, careful not to attract any attention. To fly under the radar as Colosio's successor, he was well aware of the target on his back. To emulate his boss, Miguel Trevino, he surrounded himself with a team of bodyguards who were former cops enticed by the lucrative pay offered by the Zetas. He continued with the order of business, paying off cops to keep the Zeta operations running smoothly. It helped his effort to lie low that our friends in the Mexican Army were relentless in their pursuit of all Narcos operating in the area, not only the Zetas .

Shortly after the Colosio Operation, they focused their attention on the Beltran Leyva organization and arrested the new San Pedro Plaza Boss, Rodolfo Lopez-Ibarra, alias "El Nito." El Nito, originally from Guaymas Sonora became the successor to Hector Huerta, after his arrest by our team in March. Our team made sure El Nito's reign was short-lived as they arrested him on May 18, two months after he had been named Plaza Boss and just two weeks after the Colosio operation.

El Nito was arrested at the private airport, El Aeropuerto del Norte, along with twelve other people, including two high-end prostitutes—one of them 16 years old—and his ground security team after arriving on a private Cessna from Acapulco. The Army seized numerous firearms, several hand grenades, approximately $30,000 in US dollars, 19 kilograms of marijuana, 1 kilo of cocaine, and 28 cellular phones. Following his arrest, it was discovered that El Nito had been residing in a lavish condominium located in a prestigious neighborhood of San Pedro. The condo was owned by none other than Jose "Pepe" Rojas, known as The Czar of the casinos, a notorious figure with a dark reputation as a wealthy and influential political broker. Rojas was closely affiliated with the Beltran-Leyva and Zeta cartel, further adding to his notoriety. El Nito informed our friends that during his time in Acapulco, he attended a baptism and had a personal meeting with Arturo Beltran Leyva. Leyva provided him with explicit instructions on how he wanted his operations to be executed in San Pedro. Fortunately for the citizens of San Pedro, his plans didn't pan out the way he planned, for he planned to bring violence, bloodshed, and terror to San Pedro.

Our team kept rolling along with independent intelligence from their own sources, and on June 10, 2009, two days after the Aida operation, they hit the Beltran Leyva organization again. This time taking out the most recent Plaza Boss, Omar Ibarra Lozano, "El 34," who had only been in place for a month after replacing "El Nito." Ibarra Lozano's arrest was significant as he had been a former Nuevo Leon State police officer assigned to an elite SWAT unit. Because of his unique skill set, Ibarra Lozano had been in charge of training the Beltran Leyva's sicarios, (hit men), which he conducted in the desolate mountain range of Guerrero, prior to being promoted to Plaz a Boss.

Our intelligence indicated that he had trained over 400 sicarios for the Beltran Leyva organization, known as the Fuerzas Especiales de Arturo, (FEDA), a knockoff of the Zetas, comprising rogue Federal, State and local police officers. These facts were intriguing, but what made his arrest truly captivating was the revelation of a list of 33 San Pedro police officers who were receiving payments from the Beltran Leyva cartel. According to the list, Ibarra Lozano paid each of these officers approximately $5000 pesos monthly, amounting to a total of $165,000 pesos per month. He also claimed in a statement that he collected over $100,000 monthly in extortion payoffs from various San Pedro restaurants, nightclubs and businesses. In 2009, the average exchange rate from pesos to dollars was 13.5 pesos to 1 US Dollar. The monthly payments of $165,000 to the San Pedro police amounted to around $12,222, which was a drop in the bucket for the Beltran Leyva Cartel, a real bargain in exchange for 33 police officers in your pocket. I strongly believe these estimates to be rather conservative based on some interviews I had with business owners in San Pedro. For example, one successful business owner I spoke to claimed that he was paying $100,000 pesos monthly to keep his business operating. It was the cost of doing business and could only hope that they didn't start asking for more. This is only one business owner out of hundreds of others operating successfully in San Pedro. One could easily assume that the actual figure was more in the two-million-peso range on a monthly basis, equal to roughly $148,000 US Dollars—and I feel even that figure is conservative. Whether or not the figures were accurate, the community was glad these guys were gone.

On July 13th, based on the list found on Lopez Ibarra, in an unprecedented move ever in San Pedro, the Mexican Army arrested 20 San Pedro police officers for their role in protecting the Beltran

Leyva organization. These arrests added up to 94 police officials arrested in a month in Monterrey and the surrounding cities. It was a devastating blow to the Beltran Leyva organization and also for the sterling reputation of the city of San Pedro, the Beverly Hills of Latin America; In three months, the Mexican Army had taken out three Beltran Leyva Plaza Bosses and arrested their protective forces, leaving the organization reeling in confusion and disarray and we were loving every minute.

July was a busy month, allowing Rambo to move about covertly to conduct his business. In addition to the San Pedro Police arrests, the state was having a Gubernatorial election, and the people elected Rodrigo Medina as the new governor. He promised to do his best to end corruption and violence in the state. It was big talk, despite being the youngest governor ever elected in the State of Nuevo Leon and a member of the previous governor's cabinet and political party, the PRI. However, he had failed to take action as the Zetas seized control of the entire state of Nuevo Leon. We were not big on politics. As far as we were concerned, nothing was going to change.

We kept our nose to the grindstone until we could finally pinpoint a viable location for Rambo. Rambo and Tiburon 2 handled the payoffs, but what we didn't know was where the money was stashed. It had to be a substantial sum of cash. Would they split it up between several stash houses or keep it all in one place? One thing we knew for sure, they didn't keep it in their friendly neighborhood bank. These were questions that we hoped would get answered by capturing Rambo and or Tiburon 2. Around the latter part of July, we felt we had a good location for Rambo and started planning the operation to take him down. As with the previous operations, we wanted to strike at the appropriate hour and exploit the element of surprise to its maximum potential. Things started getting more intense around the city as luck would have it, right when they were in the planning stages of the operation. For example, on the morning of August 9th, a high-profile cartel attorney, Raquenel Villanueva, was assassinated in broad daylight in the heavily populated flea market, known as the Pulga del Rio, just a few blocks away from the US Consulate by unkno wn assailants.

The story of her life unfolded like a dramatic Mexican Telenovela, with twists and turns and a complete disregard for limits or boundaries. Known as the "Iron Lawyer," Villanueva once defended Juan Garcia Abrego, the Gulf Cartel Boss now imprisoned for life in the United States. She had also recently been hired to defend Hector Huerta Rios aka "La Burra", as well as his successor, "El Nito" whom had both been recently captured by our team. She had made many enemies during her career among judges, fellow attorneys, police - officials and her clients and there had been four previous attempts on her life in the past several years. However, this time her bodyguards were of no avail, and she didn't survive.

The shooters had stealthily stalked her to the Pulga, snuck in close to her, undetected by her bodyguards, and unloaded over forty rounds in her direction from an AR-15 rifle and 9mm handguns, striking her numerous times. As she lay on the concrete floor, one gunman approached her bleeding body and fired a round into her head, making sure she would not survive this attempt. My family and I had been attending mass not too far away from the Pulga del Rio when Villanueva was killed. As we left the church, we noticed swarms of people running down the streets crying and screaming in obvious states of paranoia and despair, leaving us perplexed as to why. I didn't find out until later that Villanueva had been killed, not even fifty yards from me and my family.

Five days after Villanueva's assassination, the Zetas attacked a house in an affluent residential area of Monterrey known as Cumbres de Oro, the alleged residence of a former state police officer. Over 40 armed Zetas took part in the attack, which lasted over ninety minutes and terrorized the entire neighborhood. Twelve houses were left damaged and riddled with over 1400 rounds from various high-caliber weapons, including .50 caliber rounds. Despite receiving over 19 frantic calls for help from residents in the area, state polic e officials failed to respond, further damaging their already tarnished reputation among the community. The state, municipal and federal authorities waited until the shooting ended to respond to the pleas for help and did not show until ninety minutes after the shooting stopped, and all Zetas had fled the area. Not very reassuring in the eyes of the community, who now felt totally abandoned and left to fend for themselves by the authorities.

The terror that must have gripped these residents during this encounter is beyond my imagination. Picture the terror that grips you as your peaceful home life is shattered at three in the morning, with bullets crashing through your windows and the deafening roar of 50 caliber gunfire, while your desperate calls for help remain unanswered by those who were supposed to protect you. People felt betrayed and abandoned by the government, while helplessness and despair abounded. Public confidence in the local, state and federal authorities was virtually non-existent. It was a miracle that no casualties occurred during this attack. We only hoped that Rambo would not try to go underground and abandon his current base of operations because of these incidents.

Following the Cumbres shooting, we were overjoyed to find out that Rambo had not relocated and had remained firmly entrenched at the site we had determined to be his main operating base. The two-story house was heavily guarded and smack dab in the middle of a residential area in San Nicolas de los Garza, making the probability of collateral damage high. We were determined to avoid any harm to innocent people in this operation. Fortunately, Rambo and his crew were nocturnal, preferring to sleep during the day like cockroaches seeking refuge from the glaring sunlight, hiding in the shadows. We meticulously crafted the plan to strike Rambo's house during the serene early morning hours of Monday, August 17, when we were confident, he would be inside. The colonel ordered the troops to get a good night's rest and be ready by 3 am to prepare for the raid. He wanted them fresh, alert, and ready for battle early—so that by the time Rambo and crew hit the sack in their usual drunken state, our boys would be in a high state of readiness.

Above the rumbling of the Army jeeps plowing through the streets, there was only eerie silence. The humidity was already weighing heavy in the darkness of the new dawn. The team checked the equipment, ammo supply, and first aid kits, and supplied the radios with fresh batteries, leaving nothing else to talk about or do except focus on the operation. Due to the high population in the neighborhood, it would be nearly impossible to pull up right in front of the house because of the numerous cars parked on the side of the road, which hindered the Army vehicles from maneuvering effectively in the area. The plan was for an initial team of soldiers to insert into the neighborhood about a block away, proceed on foot to the target house. There, they would take up tactical positions around the perimeter of the house and wait for the entry team to breach the residence. All was going smooth, most of the initial perimeter team was established and were waiting for the final elements of the team to get set in place when automatic fire coming from the second floor of the house shattered the eerie quietness of the morning, sending the perimeter team scrambling for cover.

The surprise was on us this time.

We had not expected them to be awake at this hour, but they were, and they were firing away with bad intentions. Just when we seemed to regain some sense of control over the situation, someone threw a fragmentation grenade in the direction of the team situated near a fence closest to the house. The flash lit up the darkness and the concussive effect of the explosion shook the ground, shattering the windows of various vehicles parked on the sidewalk, and starting a cacophonous orchestra of shrill car alarms. Shards of hot piercing shrapnel sprayed the immediate area, hitting three of our guys, leaving them writhing in pain on the asphalt, while bullets rained down from the second-story window in an attempt to finish them off. Our team immediately returned fire and a group of fellow soldiers scurried to assist our fallen team members and extracted them to safety.

The gunfire intensified as our team started taking up positions on the rooftops of neighboring houses to get a more accurate view of the second level of the target house. The gunfire stopped for a moment as Rambo's crew regrouped and reloaded. Our team did not let up however, and at this point one of our team members, positioned himself in front of the house and fired a perfect shot from his grenade launcher right into the second-story window creating an infernal blast that seemed to shake the roof off its rafters and rattle the foundations of the neighboring houses. Chaotic screaming emanated from the house as a black cloud of smoke from a fire caused by the explosion billowed into the fresh morning air.

We were on the offensive now.

Our team kept peppering the house with gunfire, all the while moving closer, in an effort to gain entry into the inferno. A group of three Zetas gave up the fight and fled the burning house from the rooftop. They vaulted onto the roofs of several neighboring houses and holed up in one to take their last stand. As the team moved in, they heard women screaming from within the residence, and a man's voice told them to back off because they had two women hostages.

"Don't be cowards! Let the women go! They are innocent and have nothing to do with this situation. You are completely surrounded, and you have nowhere to go!"

"Fuck you assholes! We are getting out of this alive and taking them with us!"

"Don't be stupid! You have no way out! Don't let them die because of your decision! Let them return to their families!"

The women were screaming hysterically. Three team members approached the house from the rear and entered through an open garage door, giving the point man a clear visual of the hostage taker. He signaled to his fellow team members and took close aim. Above the wailing of the hostages, a single shot rang out piercing the hostage taker through the right eye socket and spraying blood, brains and bone matter throughout the house. The team then tossed a concussion grenade into the house, causing the remaining Zetas to scurry outside, firing their weapons in a futile attempt to escape.

They were met with a barrage of gunfire, which ended the hostage situation, the horrific gunfight, and the life of El Rambo.

After the gunfight, our team received information from one of the five arrestees that Rambo had a safe house in Guadalupe, Nuevo Leon. Our team hit that house as well and arrested another eight people after a short gunfight. All-in-all, the operation resulted in the arrest of thirteen people and forensics confirmed that one of the four dead in the shootout was indeed El Rambo, whose true name is Refugio Garza Pescador. Among the documentary evidence collected, our team found a notebook with entries detailing troop and Federal Police movements and a plan to break out and rescue their old pal Aida, aka "La Guera", from prison. Seized from both houses were many high caliber rifles, fragmentation grenades, six armored vehicles, t-shirts with the lettering Fuerzas Especiales de Sierra Nectar, (Sierra Nectar being a moniker for San Nicolas), more shirts with the insignia AFI (Federal Police) and many cell phones.

The gunfight wounded five of our boys, with two of them being seriously injured, but they were expected to survive. The entire gunfight lasted over two hours, leaving the surrounding neighborhood looking like a World War II combat zone. Miraculously, the gunfight didn't cause any harm to civilians. Although we were disappointed that we hadn't found the money stash we hoped Rambo would be keeping, we successfully eliminated him, along with most of his minions, one of whom was later identified as a former member of the Nuevo Leon State police SWAT team.

We felt like we were gaining ground after the success of the Rambo operation and we had faith that if we kept up the pressure, we would get Miguel Trevino soon. We still had plenty of work to do, and as soon as we planted Rambo in the ground, we began planning our next operation on El Tiburon 2, hoping to find the elusive Zeta money.

Chapter 12: Shark Hunt

Saul Bonifacio Martinez, aka "El Tiburon" (The Shark), was a former police officer who went rogue and started working for the Zetas while he was still an active member of the Santa Catarina Police Department. In 2007, while still working as a police officer for Santa Catarina, Tiburon and another officer got arrested for their involvement in the kidnapping of two individuals. Not surprisingly, the court dismissed his case and released him shortly thereafter because of lack of evidence. Is that surprising? Kidnapping for profit was his specialty, and as bad as it sounds, his passion. There is no way to count how many people he victimized, tortured, and killed. His nickname fit the bill, The Shark. He preyed on innocent citizens, using force and intimidation on anyone who stood in his way. A tactic he likely used to get his case dismissed.

El Tiburon felt invincible, and sources told us he routinely mocked SEDENA during Zeta gatherings, frequently shouting expletives at them, such as, "SEDENA me la pela!!" (SEDENA jerks me off). We were certainly up to the challenge, and we knew that capturing Tiburon might give us valuable clues we needed to get to Heriberto Lazcano, Miguel Trevino and his brother Omar or lead us to their ever-elusive money stash.

Each case presents unique challenges that require careful consideration. In this situation, the difficulty arose from Tiburon's near-constant mobility. Whenever he chose to stay in one place, a security radius constantly surrounded him, ensuring that he was warned of any potential enforcement threats. Having observed the carelessness of his predecessors, he adopted a cautious and security-conscious mindset. He spent most of his time near the lake in Santiago, where locals once enjoyed family time, boat rides, swimming and other aquatic activities, before Tiburon and Rambo took over the area. As was becoming commonplace, after the Zetas invasion, these activities diminished significantly. Visitors were scarce and traffic was slower, making it easier to spot surveillance vehicles or individuals that did not fit in the area. Our team faced the daunting challenge of infiltrating El Tiburon's rings of security without being detected, launching the enforcement operation quickly and efficiently, and extracting from the area before Zeta reinforcements could arrive.

Any such operation seemed like an almost impossible task, where we would need the services of Sir James Bond or maybe Mission Impossible's Ethan Hunt and crew. Unfortunately, Hunt and Bond were not available—so, no Martinis shaken, not stirred, and no Jack Harmon providing cool tech stuff for our mission. Tiburon's security perimeter comprised three rings, which we referred to as a three-ring circus. The outermost ring could be as far away as two miles from the boss, depending on the area; the second ring would be in a tighter area, maybe a mile or half a mile from the boss; and the third ring was physically with and in visual contact with the boss.

The first and outermost ring of the perimeter, operated by halcones (lookouts), comprised municipal police, taxi drivers and street urchins, provided primary intelligence regarding potential threats directly to the leader of the second ring. Any suspicious activity or anything out of place was immediately reported to the leader of the second ring. The second ring comprised what are called estacas (stacks), which comprised about six heavily armed men per vehicle, usually in four pickup trucks or Suburban SUV type vehicles—twenty-four men. The estacas were proven members of the Zetas who had worked their way up the ladder through displays of courage and reliability in battle, whether against law enforcement or rival cartels. The leader of the second ring is the leader of the entire security force, as his decisions affect the actions of the entire security team. Once he received intelligence regarding a potential threat, he immediately reported to the third ring to alert them of the threat and then decided whether to confront the threat or issue the order to remove or extract the Plaza Boss from the area. The third ring was the last line of defense for the Plaza Boss and comprised the most highly trusted estacas. They were his pretorian guard and held his life in their hands. The function of the inner ring was two-fold: to protect the boss at all costs and to safely extract him from a violent confrontation. When the order to extract was given, they were to split the team into two halves. One half of the team was to deploy in order to support the second ring in case of a confrontation, while the other half of the team was to extract the Plaza Boss from the area and take him to a safe house. They were well organized and highly vigilant. To make matters worse, Tiburon was paranoid and rarely used his phone, frequently turning it off, which made it difficult for us to track and establish a pattern of life. The only constant in the equation was that he liked to hang around in a specific area of the lake on Friday evening s and weekends.

   This was one of our toughest cases, and our team met frequently to brainstorm on operational strategy. Weekends at the lake seemed to be the only opportunity we would have to execute any action against him. Tiburon was paranoid because of the successful operations against his buddies, Colosio, Aida and Rambo. He knew he had a target on his back and did not want the same results to befall him, so we had to have a perfect plan. We considered an aerial assault with helicopters and the team repelling into a drop zone, but the risk outweighed the gains, the choppers would be spotted, and Tiburon would be whisked away immediately, and our boys would be subject to an unnecessary confrontation, with little ground support. We considered launching several boats from a discreet launching dock on the lake, but that measure would be too high profile, and our team would be spotted before they ever disembarked to launch the operation, exposing them to great risk. Our brainstorming meetings were volatile and tense because we wanted to take him out as soon as possible, but we also wanted to conduct the operation with the odds stacked in our favor, or at the very minimum, fifty-fifty; We felt we could win at fifty-fifty odds. We spent many hours discussing strategy, safety and effectiveness. No matter how tense and highly argumentative these meetings were, we all had one common goal. Capture Tiburon and bring our boys back safely. We threw out the idea of the trojan horse strategy for discussion, and it reminded me of my days as a young undercover agent in McAllen, Texas, when we effectively used it for undercover operations. In McAllen, many times in undercover roles, we posed as marijuana suppliers with buyers from Houston, Louisiana, or Dallas. Once the buyers showed us they had the money to purchase the load, we would drive up in an old Chevy van that was supposed to contain their marijuana order, but was manned by an arrest team of six DEA agents—Surprise! Surprise !

The trojan horse strategy could work if planned creatively. We thought about tractor trailers or moving vans, but those vehicles would seem out of place in Santiago and would most certainly catch the attention of the security rings. We contemplated organizing a mock funeral procession, but the sheer number of vehicles required, and the lack of feasibility prevented us from pursuing it. Fortunately for us, we had a brilliant young lieutenant on our team who was highly resourceful. The day after we had the all-night discussion on strategy and infiltrating Tiburon's ring of security, the Lieutenant came up with an incredible out-of-the-box idea. Turns out that the Lieutenant had convinced his church, "La Fuerza de Cristo," (The strength of Christ), to lend him three twelve-passenger vans for a supposed outing. How he convinced the pastor in to lending him the vans? I do not know or care to know. In each van, we could pack ten soldiers, a driver and a team leader, riding shotgun. That could infiltrate Tiburon's security rings with no problem; as long as Tiburon's security actually believed that the occupants were a group, out for a weekend excursion at the lake in Santiago, we would be gol den.

The only other tactical problem was the extraction of the team, if indeed the team could successfully infiltrate the security rings and get to El Tiburon. We all knew if the entry team was successful, all hell was going to break loose and the outer rings would immediately fall in to assist Tiburon, which would expose our team to more risk. But we figured thirty special forces guys in three vans, with the element of surprise, should be able to hold their own until reinforcements arrived. Geography played a role in our favor as well. There was only one main road coming into or out of Santiago and that was the Carretera Nacional, which flowed east to west from Ciudad Victoria,

Tamaulipas, all the way to San Pedro Garza Garcia, Nuevo Leon, both ends which would be covered by small advance teams. To the North, any escape route was hindered naturally by the voluminous Lake Santiago and a steep mountainous range beyond the lake, and any attempted escape route to the south through the town of Santiago would be severely hindered by the brutal and unforgiving Sierra Madre mountains. Tiburon and his security team had unwittingly committed a critical tactical error by choosing this location as his safe-haven, which was basically a small strip of land near the lake. In doing so, he had set himself up in an ideal choke point, leaving him and his team vulnerable to a measured and calculated attack. We would use his own comfort zone to our advantage, tactically.

Positioned at the airport, SEDENA had a pair of helicopters on standby. In a mere five minutes, they could reach the target location, prepared to offer firepower and prevent any potential escape. SEDENA also had a team of forty more soldiers stationed at a location that was far enough away from the operation to not be seen as a threat by Tiburon's security, but close enough to reach the scene within a maximum of fifteen minutes. Fifteen minutes seems like a lifetime when all hell is breaking loose, but in this case, there was no other option. We felt confident with the plan and waited to put it in motion once we knew Tiburon was at his apparent favorite place on Fridays, totally relaxed, and feeling safe in his comfort zone.

As with any plan, something is always bound to go wrong. After devising the initial plan, we carefully considered all the potential pitfalls and challenges that could arise. After reviewing the aerial photos of the suspected target location, we became uneasy about the prospect of leaving the entry team vulnerable for fifteen minutes without proper backup. We were concerned that if the entry team somehow got caught and trapped between the two initial security rings, we would suffer severe casualties. To ensure the safety of the entry team, we made a quick adjustment to our plan. Once the entry team notified us that they were within five minutes of the first security ring, we coordinated for the back-up team of forty soldiers and helicopters to start advancing towards the confirmed target area. That would cut down the entry team's exposure once the bullets began to fly, and we knew they would. As with any tactical operation, we wanted to tip the odds in our favor. We all felt comfortable with the revised plan. Now we just had to wait for confirmation that Tiburon would show up at his favorite Friday spot, a popular seafood restaurant known as La Playa, which had a beautiful lakeside view.

For days, I could not sleep, thinking and overthinking the plan. I have never been a smoker, but during that time frame, I think I indulged in a few cigarettes and more than a couple of tequilas and beers to take the edge off and keep my sanity. In the end, we had confidence in our team. They were SEDENA Special Forces—the best of the best, committed and dedicated to avenging the deaths of their nine comrades, who were murdered by the hands of the Zetas. On Friday September 4, 2009, at approximately 9:30 PM, Tiburon's phone pinged at his favorite Friday place and the plan was set in motion.

Our first call was to the pilots to inform them to get flight ready. The mission was imminent, and they needed time to go through their protocols before taking off. To give the appearance of normalcy and routine, the forty soldiers on the ground team had been standing by, near their rendezvous point for several days, in anticipation of the call. They were locked and loaded, ready to proceed to the target when called. The entry team was given the green light and proceeded to the location. We updated each other regularly on Tiburon's whereabouts, and the signal remained stable the whole time. He remained rooted in his spot at La Playa—it was game on! All systems go. I prayed several Hail Marys as the plan unfolded. At approximately 10:30 PM, the entry team in the "Fuerza de Cristo Vans" excitedly announced their proximity to the first ring by exclaiming, "Estamos a cinco!" We are five minutes out.

Aware of the Zetas and potentially corrupt cops monitoring SEDENA's frequencies, we minimized our radio traffic. And, in the briefings before the operation, "Estamos a cinco," was a code we set up to inform the pilots and the forty-member backup team it was time to move to the target location. After what seemed like an eternity, the entry team announced, "uno logrado!" (One accomplished)—our code to indicate that they had penetrated the first ring of security. "enterado" (roger), responded the chopper team and the forty-member back-up team. Radio silence and code usage was a critical part of the plan to keep the entry team covert. Meanwhile, Tiburon's location was stationary at La Playa. He was probably having a good old time, completely unaware of what was coming, enjoying the moment, laughing it up and boozing it up with not a care in the world. After all, to his way of thinking, he had the best security team in Mexico. "Segundo logrado" (second accomplished). The second security ring had been infiltrated without a problem. Now it was all upon the grace of God to keep our boys safe as they entered the combat zone, where death surely awaited.

During Operation Desert storm, a tactical principal known as "shock and awe" was applied by US coalition troops to defeat Iraqi forces. As explained by the authors Harlan K. Ullman and James P. Wade in their book, *Shock and Awe-Achieving Rapid Dominance* "the objective of the shock and awe principal is to seize control of the environment and paralyze or so overload an adversary's perceptions and understanding of events that the enemy would be incapable of resistance at the tactical and strategic levels, effectively rendering the enemy's ability to fight useless and most importantly, destroying their will to fight." As the team approached the last ring of security, they all had this concept in mind—speed, surprise, and violence of action! The concept had worked in Iraq and we were about to use it on the Zetas.

Tiburon's team never knew what hit them. It took Tiburon's security team valuable seconds to even register what was happening, as our team pulled up to the La Playa Bar and jumped out of the church vans, armed to the teeth. By the time they realized what was happening, two of them were already dead on the ground and one took off running for cover, abandoning the fight completely. Chaos ensued as the two choppers, having timed the assault perfectly, buzzed the area like mad hornets looking for runaway stragglers and to prevent a rear assault by the second ring on our team, the whump of the rotor blades creating a deafening roar. The situation became difficult to manage as terrified innocent bystanders ran for cover creating mass confusion.

Tiburon and one of his bodyguards used the confusion to attempt to escape the assault, jumped into a white GMC pickup and revved it in reverse in a desperate attempt to flee. The truck fishtailed in the gravel bed and swung out of control, violently crashing into a large oak tree. Our team converged on the truck as Tiburon's bodyguard jumped out and starting firing indiscriminately at our team, taking a last desperate stand for his boss, but he was no match for the Special Forces as both he and Tiburon spent their last seconds of life on earth in a state of horrified disbelief, before being killed in the barrage of Special Forces bullets. After the shooting stopped, four of Tiburon's bodyguards lay dead on the ground and another was found cowering, wounded under a pickup truck at the scene, and one had fled, and successfully mixed into the crowd of onlookers and disappeared. Our boys decimated Tiburon's entire estaca before they even knew what was happening. Two of our boys were wounded, as well, but did not receive life threatening injuries. Shock and Awe had worked to perfection. The second ring did not even try to come to Tiburon's rescue. Either they were so intimidated by the show of force—or they were too embarrassed to face their peers after failing to detect the assault team. They plainly lost their will to fight!

The victory over Tiburon's team was short lived and bittersweet, because a stray bullet had struck and killed an innocent bystander. In a selfless act of heroism, the young man, to protect his younger brother from the gunfire, had shielded him by throwing him to the ground and lying on top of him as the shootout took place. Unfortunately, he was hit and passed away, completing his mission of saving his little brother's life and died a hero.

The wounded Zeta provided our team with crucial information that required immediate action. The coward gave our team the address for the safehouse that Tiburon had been using. Wanting to press our advantage, and keep up momentum, our team immediately deployed to the house to search for evidence or more of Tiburon's associates. But the house was empty, except for one kidnap victim whom Tiburon and his gang had held captive for over a month. Pretending to be a Zeta, this local business executive had been extorting fees from other business people in the area. They held him captive as punishment for impersonating a Zeta and subjected him to daily beatings with the famous tabla. He was definitely happy to see our team that day.

The house was Tiburon's version of the House of hell. Our team found chains, bloody tablas and sledgehammers used to torture kidnap victims, bloody garments, 6 AR-15s, pistols, fragmentation grenades, bullet-proof vests, over 2000 rounds of ammunition and numerous cellphones, and Nextel radios. Most importantly, they found 10 notebooks containing a list of names of corrupt cops on the payroll, covered payments made to cops from 9 different municipalities in the Nuevo Leon citric region, including the Santiago Chief of police and his top commander. Finding narco-lists of this magnitude became the norm during operations and subsequent searches. It was mind-boggling.

While we were busy sifting through the evidence, the team interrogating the cowardly bodyguard was meticulously reviewing his late boss's activities, focusing on cash transactions. Although he did not say much, he gave up the name of an accountant he knew only as El Jorge whom Tiburon talked to frequently. That was all we needed. Our team immediately started the arduous task of going through each phone used by Tiburon, Rambo, Colosio, and Aida looking for any and every single Jorge we could find. It was like putting a giant puzzle together as each one of these bosses had multiple phones and used codewords for specific people. Jorge is a very common name and the time we put in attempting to get a viable option was extremely challenging—a challenge solved with the application of technology.

After finding over twenty Jorges in various cell phones and examining the cell tower data, it became evident that calls to J1 and Jota1 were consistently originating from a specific cell tower in the upscale Cumbres neighborhood of Monterrey. After looking at call histories from these cellphones, our analysts pinpointed a possible new number for Jota1. We immediately started tracking the phone, even though we didn't know who was holding it. After diligently tracking the phone for several days, we had amassed a wealth of data on its movements and call history. It was apparent that Jota1 was calling some of the same numbers from the seized phone.

The pattern of life we developed put the phone at a large house at 6627 Cuidad de Malaga, Colonia Cumbres, Monterrey. The house was an upscale two-story mansion, with a well-kept lawn. Our tracking devices showed that the phone of interest was inside. We hit the house and on September 23, 2009, at approximately 5:00 am. Our team made entry without a single shot being fired. What we discovered in the residence left us in shock, surpassing most other seizures we had so far encountered.

We hit the mother lode—in terms of the Zetas elusive money. The house was filled with stacks of envelopes, each one stuffed with cash, destined for police officials at every level in the State of Nuevo Leon. We discovered a new narco list containing the names of over 500 influential police and government officials. Among them were members of the State Police Homicide Unit, the renowned Anti-Kidnapping Unit, as well as municipal and federal police officers who were all implicated in receiving bribes from the Zetas.

The discovery made my head spin at the size and scope of the operation. It registered with me then that we could trust no one. Everyone seemed to take some piece of the Zeta money. They arranged money counters all over the house for efficient counting and disbursement of Zeta proceeds to the proper authorities. We had just knocked one of the Zeta's main accounting departments out of commission. After all the counting was done, the total amount of money

seized amounted to $73 million pesos—the US equivalent of roughly
$5,455,904 US dollars—$3.7 million of which was in US dollars, the
rest in Mexican pesos. Miguel Trevino, wherever he could be now,
was going to be pissed. No matter how much protection money he
doled out, it seemed to have no effect. Within a month, we successfully
eliminated Rambo, Tiburon, and their entire accounting cell, crip-
pling their operation. We also seized a substantial amount of their
illicit funds and uncovered many corrupt officials on their payroll
throughout Nuevo Leon. I would have given anything to see the
reaction on his face when he found out that we seized more than $5
million of his dollars. I am convinced that he ordered the execution
of several people that night whether they deserved it or not.

In the end, corruption had lost on these particular days. Miguel
Trevino and the Zetas had to be realizing that no amount of money
paid to corrupt cops or officials could deter us. We were determined
to locate him and eliminate him. We were going to catch him sooner
than later—and, like his companions, it would be when he least
expected it.

Chapter 13: Game Changer

Geoffrey Chaucer is credited with the quote "all good things must come to an end." In stark contrast to Chaucer's quote, I once had a boss who, as a young DEA Agent, gave me advice that was both unforgettable and laced with colorful language. I had been part of a successful Task Force group, where I had the luxury of picking my cases for many years. However, our office was expanding, and now they tasked me with mentoring lesser experienced agents in the Enforcement Groups. I did not want to leave my old reliable group and be thrown into the role of mentor, so I immediately expressed my displeasure about the decision to my boss.

I will never forget his response as he deadpanned from behind his huge oak desk, somehow resembling the Great and Powerful OZ. He said, with an East Coast accent, "Leo, working for DEA is like working for a whorehouse, the better you are the more you get screwed."

I had no response to his explanation and just accepted my fate. I left his office laughing. His quote remains with me over 25 years later, and probably still rings true. As we advanced with our goal to capture Miguel Trevino, Chaucer's and my old boss' sayings kept ringing true for us. The GOPES started out strong and conducted several successful missions on the targets we provided for them. They were so successful that someone in a high-ranking position put the brakes on them and disbanded the team, promoting several key members to different regions of the country. The same thing was happening to our SEDENA team. Their success with their operations caught the interest of high-ranking members of SEDENA in Mexico City and, knowingly or unknowingly, dismantled them. The Colonel in charge of our team was promoted to Brigadier General in Mexico City. The lieutenant, whom we had befriended and who had become our biggest ally, also received a promotion and was reassigned as an instructor to the Military College in Mexico City. Their replacements did not have the same goals and enthusiasm as our friends did, and we noticed the change as soon as they left.

Just like a sports team, The Zetas have a next man up policy. Their next man up in Monterrey made one wonder where Trevino and associates could find such vile characters with such apparent ease. Ricardo Almanza-Morales was one of four brothers, all nicknamed "Los Goris" short for Gorillas. Mexican culture is notorious for finding humor among the darkest of topics and whoever nicknamed these four brothers was spot on, because their resemblance to gorillas was uncanny—no offense meant to the gorillas in the wild. All four of the brothers moved up in the Zeta leadership structure because of their loyalty to Trevino and mostly because of their fearless nature and propensity for violence.

The Gori brothers each had their specific call signs: Ricardo Almanza-Morales Gori-1; Raymundo Almanza-Morales, Gori-2; Eduardo Almanza-Morales, Gori-3; and Octavio Almanza-Morales, Gori-4. That all four brothers dedicated themselves to a life of crime and violence is intriguing. How did their parents raise these guys, and what values were taught to them, if any? There is not much information on their background, but all of them turned out to be hardened criminals. Most children in Mexico with limited resources learn to survive on the streets at a very young age, or else they go hungry. Their only hope is their survival skills. The only way to survive on the street is often to take what you want from others. I can only imagine family gatherings or birthday celebrations at the Gori brother's household—maybe a live kidnap victim as a pinata for the kids? And then what about the dinner conversations? Maybe it went something like this:

Gori-4: "Yeah I chopped this guy's fingers off today. What did you do today, bro?"

Gori-3: "Is that all? I cut this guy's tongue off, threw it on the grill and made him eat it."

Gori-2: "I chopped this one guy's legs off and then beat the shit out of his brother with one of his legs."

Gori-1: "Well, I cut this one guy's eyeballs out and made him eat them."

I'll leave the rest of the hypothetical conversation to your imaginations. The point is, not only were these guys bad, but they were also true psychopaths. Not a single one of them displayed any emotion or empathy. I would say that is an extremely powerful genetic trait and Miguel Trevino, the ultimate Zeta scout, had an eye for recognizing and recruiting these types of individuals.

The Gori brothers had been on our radar for some time already, but we were busy and tied up with other operations. However, after the Tiburon operation, they became the focus of our attention especially Gori-1, Ricardo Almanza-Morales, who had recently inherited the Monterrey Plaza after the deaths of Rambo and El Tiburon. As soon as he got into power, he started re-establishing the rule and control-by-fear method that the Zetas had mastered over the years, and on November 4th, promptly assassinated Brigadier General Juan Arturo Esparza Cantu.

The General had just received his appointment as Chief of Police of Garcia, Nuevo Leon, only four days before his murder. El Gori was sending a message to the community that the Zetas were still in power and would not let a setback to their organization deter them from carrying out their nefarious plans in the region. Gori-1 was following a plan designed by his brother, Gori-4, who had previously killed Brigadier General Mauro Enrique Tello Quinones in Cancun Quintana Roo, shortly after his appointment as Chief of Police in Cancun, earlier in the year.

True to form, SEDENA is a brotherhood, and their members are highly loyal and will never let an attack on one of their own go unpunished. Six days after General Tello's murder, SEDENA captured Gori-4. One brother down, three more to go. Our intelligence revealed that Gori 2 was put in charge of operations for the Zetas in Guatemala and Belize to oversee ton-shipments of cocaine coming into Central America from Colombia and Peru and provide safe passage for those loads to Mexico. We believe they appointed him as the Plaza Boss of the region shortly after the Colosio operation. He never got a chance to enjoy his reign because SEDENA captured him on May 20, shortly after he arrived in Monterrey.

Two brothers down. Two to go.

Our focus was mainly on Gori-1, as he was the new Plaza Boss in the area. After the murder of General Esparza-Cantu, we received intelligence that Gori-1 had fled to the border town of Reynosa, Tamaulipas, to hide out for a while. He still called the shots in Monterrey, and he was extremely cautious, especially after SEDENA or the Federal Police had captured or killed his brothers and so many of his cohorts. When he wasn't hiding out, he traveled in convoys of over thirty vehicles—mostly SUVs—back and forth from Monterrey to Reynosa.

Despite all his precautions, we located a ranch where he usually stayed when he was in Monterrey. It was a large horse ranch, formerly used by Miguel Trevino to train and maintain his prized horses. The ranch was difficult to locate from the road, well hidden from traffic and highly guarded. Fortunately, it was located approximately ten miles from SEDENA's base of operations in Escobedo. We were ecstatic because if we determined he was there, the reaction time would be quick—or so we thought.

We received intelligence that Gori-1 was definitely at the ranch and that he had remained stationary for a good while. As I mentioned at the beginning of this chapter, the team we were using comprised of different personnel and leadership, who had different philosophies than our original core team. When we passed along the information to the new team, they showed a total lack of enthusiasm. Gori-1 stayed at the ranch for three days straight, and nothing was done.

When we asked about their hesitation, the commander told us that the operation was too dangerous because Gori's people were heavily armed, and he did not want to take on the risk. The Special Forces commander was telling us they did not want to take a risk on a target who killed a former general? Special Forces? Seriously? We were extremely disappointed and dumbfounded by the logic, but there was nothing we could do. It was his call not ours. I really had to respect his decision. We both knew that if we planned it right, we could minimize or even avoid casualties. But he did not want the responsibility or run the risk of sustaining casualties, and I could not disagree, but as I said before it was his call; they were his troops, his country and, although disappointed, I understood.

We were in quite a predicament. We couldn't even say we were back to square one because, in reality, all the squares had vanished from the game. The Federal Police would not do it, and now SEDENA, our trusted go-to team, did not want to take the risk. We could not even think of mentioning anything about our intelligence to the State police because many of them were on the Zetas payroll. Our predicament was beyond frustrating; it was a maddening ordeal, compounded by the relentless ticking of the clock. Gori-1 preferred being mobile and never stayed for too long in one place, and the clock ran out on our window of opportunity. After spending five days at the ranch, Gori-1 disappeared, leaving us completely clueless about his whereabouts.

It was truly disheartening that we had squandered a golden opportunity to capture such a villainous individual. A ruthless murderer was roaming the streets looking for more victims while we twiddled our thumbs, trying to find a solution. It bothered me to feel so powerless and dejected, but there was nothing me or anyone in DEA could do. It was a bad day. It seemed like everyone, every situation, and every circumstance were conspiring against us. Feeling dejected, frustrated, and pissed off, we distracted ourselves from our predicament by engaging in what most DEA agents excelled at: unwinding with a few drinks! After all, it was Friday night.

Monterrey is one of the most sophisticated and cosmopolitan cities in Mexico, offering many entertainment options for tourists and locals. For a team of pissed off DEA agents, we found our solace in a musty old downtown cantina, El Rancho, that featured a live band playing classic rock. It was the perfect place to take our minds off our frustrations.

Buckets of ice-cold beer flowed smoothly as we partook of some of the best bar food on the planet, such as "Atropellado" (Road-kill), which comprises dried beef sauteed in light oil, mixed with serrano chile, onions, garlic, all smothered in tomato-based salsa. The dish is served with avocado slices on the side and freshly mad e fluffy-soft flour tortillas with just the right amount of spiciness to keep you ordering beer all night long. They also served "Frijoles con Veneno" (Beans with poison), which comprises refried beans mixed with shredded pork roast and sizzling hot salsa al molcajete (mortar and pestle) which one eats with freshly made fried tortilla chips. Like crack cocaine, the dish is simply addictive, irresistible and keeps one mindlessly ordering bucket after bucket of cold beer.

The band pounded out The Hollies' famous song, "Long cool woman in a Black Dress;" Creedence Clearwater Revival's "Have you ever seen the rain," The Zombie's "Time of the Season," as well as songs by the Eagles, Santana, and Van Halen, among others. To add to the ambience of the bar and as a reminder that one was still in Mexico, a mariachi band played traditional Mexican songs when-ever the rock group took its break. Songs such as "Mexico Lindo," "Guadalajara," and "La Feria de las Flores" inspired us to order round after round of tequila shots, as shouts of "Viva Mexico!" melded into the background with the vibrant mariachi music. The night slowly ebbed into the early morning hours of the next day.

The party was finally over, leaving us with pounding headaches and the lingering weight of our problem. We had no actionable team to take on the Gori operation. Adding to our dilemma, Gori's where-abouts remained a complete mystery to us. We were out of options.

I called up one of my team members and we met at a hole in the wall restaurant near the US Consulate, that specialized in menudo, the holy grail for all hangovers. You haven't truly experienced culinary bliss until you savor a piping hot bowl of menudo from Menudo Don Luis in Monterrey. Pair it with some barbacoa tacos, generously topped with a fiery habanero salsa that will jolt your taste buds awake. To cool down the heat, quench your thirst with a refreshing lemonade made with zesty, hand-squeezed limes and sparkling mineral water. It just does not get any better.

The place was packed as usual, even more so on this cold gloomy November day. My partner and I ate in silence as we contemplated our situation and waited for the misty fog to clear from the space in our minds and bring back a sense of functionality to our reasoning. We paid our tab and walked the short distance to the US Consulate to brainstorm about the operation, picking up some coffee and some hot freshly made empanadas de cajeta (baked pastry coated with sugar and cinnamon and stuffed with caramel) from a cheerful street vendor along the way. He was young and full of spirit, embarking on his first entrepreneurial venture, totally oblivious to the dangers the Zetas brought to the streets of Monterrey.

As we walked away, I thought about how this young man was just trying to put food on the table for his family and how unconscionable it was for the Zetas to just come in and take it away. Monterrey is beyond comparison; the quality of life should be first class. But the Zetas created an environment where the people of Monterrey lived in terror, afraid of going out to their favorite restaurants, bars, parks, or hangouts. Ruthless people Lazcano, Z-40, Gori, Canicon, El Tiburon, and others perpetuated it. Worse yet, the police did nothing about it—as much a part of the problem as the Zetas themselves. I wanted this guy off the street. But no matter how much we brainstormed, the fact is we did not know where he was. Even if we found him, we had no team to go after him.

Having no other reasonable option, we gave it a couple of days to see if he surfaced again. Time was our enemy. The following week was Thanksgiving week for us and after that, the Christmas holidays would be upon us. In Mexico, the Christmas Holidays officially begin on December 12, the day of the Virgin de Guadalupe, and the y officially end on January 6, known as Dia de los Reyes or Three Kings Day. Mexicans typically refer to this extended vacation span as "Lupe-Reyes." Everyone would soon be gone on "Lupe-Reyes" vacation, including the bad guys. In the meantime, our options were minimal.

We had three options: either convince the commander to conduct the operation, search for another team capable of taking action, or hope for a miracle before "Lupe-Reyes" began. I wanted to go on "Lupe-Reyes" vacation too. But I wanted to do it, secure knowing that Gori was off the streets for good. For now, I was going to return to Texas, enjoy the Thanksgiving Holidays, spend some quality time with family, and pray for a miracle.

Thanksgiving, one of my favorite holidays, is a time to reflect on our blessings and express gratitude. Personally, it serves as a time for introspection and self-evaluation. It gives me the opportunity to reconnect with myself spiritually, and also to reconnect with family and old friends. Out of the blue one morning, I received a call from a colleague who was a DEA supervisor in McAllen, Texas. We met for lunch to discuss old times and catch up on the latest news. I am not a fan of cliches, but I am also someone who doesn't believe in coincidences. I can still hear the words of my old partner, Mario

Alvarez, echoing in my mind: "It is better to be lucky than good."
Today, that cliché—coincidence, if you prefer that term—was in full
effect. It turns out that my friend had a close relationship with a
SEMAR captain who was based in Matamoros, Tamaulipas.

SEMAR is an acronym for Secretaría de la Marina, the Mexican
Marines. According to my friend, the captain commanded a special
forces unit of forty marines, who had been deployed to Matamoros.
They were eager to enter the action against any cartel member that
was deemed valuable. In all my time with DEA, I had never heard
of the Mexican Marines being part of any inland anti-narcotics operations, so I was skeptical. When I was stationed in Guadalajara,
Mexico, we collaborated with a unit of the Marines, but only for
maritime operations. My friend assured me that this Special Forces
unit of SEMAR was highly capable of performing inland operations
and that most of the unit had received training by the US Navy
SEALS, the most elite military unit in the world. The best part about
this Special Forces SEMAR team is that all team members were from
out of state. No team member was from Nuevo Leon or Tamaulipas,
and they did not have any familial ties in either state, so they could
not be extorted with threats to family members or associates. There
was truly nothing for us to lose. We could not have asked for a better s
cenario.

We would launch a surprise attack on the Zetas using a Special
Forces team that received direct training from US Navy SEALS,
catching them completely off guard. This relationship could prove to
be groundbreaking. It was all I could do to keep my composure and
stop myself from jumping out of my chair and squeezing my friend
to death in a bear hug. This was the answer we had been desperately
searching for, and it seemed too perfect to be mere happenstance.

I told him we in Monterrey were interested in working with them. He got the captain on the phone, and we made plans to meet in Monterrey when I returned from Thanksgiving vacation. This had to be divine intervention, or dumb luck. Regardless, luck or divine intervention—it made no difference. Whatever it was, I was going to take this ball and run with it. Whenever luck turns in your favor, take it! The bad guys always did! It was time for us to start doing some tak ing as well!

The excitement in the chill December air was like an opening day of football season in Texas and it was hard to contain our excitement and enthusiasm. A certain element of electricity filled the icy chill in the December air and our expectations were high. Cautious, but high. A sort of cautious optimism. This unit, although highly trained and capable had not been tested. On our side, though, was that the Zetas had no clue what was coming, and in the past, there was always the danger of information being leaked. Not this time. The team was working on this operation solo. No Federal Police. No local Army. They did not even tell us what time the operation would take place. All they asked from us was to keep updating them on Gori's status.

Our intelligence indicated that Gori was hiding in a secluded Quinta, surrounded by the tranquil beauty of Monterrey's iconic Cerro del Silla (Saddleback Mountain). The Cerro de la Silla, part of the Sierra Madre Occidental, is an iconic landmark synonymous with Monterrey and the State of Nuevo Leon. With its impressive altitude of nearly 6000 feet, the mountain can be spotted and appreciated from different locations across the State of Nuevo Leon. El Cerro de la Silla has been the subject of an infinite number of photographs, with the sunrise and moonrise serving as a backdrop, homage to its immense beauty. Coincidentally, Gori's Quinta was situated near the Quinta where authorities apprehended former Gulf Cartel Plaza Boss, Juan Garcia Abrego, in 1996. The Quinta was in an extremely secluded area, surrounded by breathtaking views of the Cerro de la Silla, though I seriously doubt El Gori took time out to admire the view of the Cerro and the sunrise from his hideaway. Funny thing is, he should have. He also should have paid heed to another cliché I'd come to embrace: "Live life as though this were your last day on ear th."

In his case, it would be his last day on earth, his last sunrise he would ever get to see and his last chance to appreciate the majestic beauty of El Cerro de la Silla.

In the early morning hours of a cold December 4, a team of eight marines were helicoptered into the frigid, jungle-like mountainside of El Cerro de la Silla. They stealthily trekked several miles through densely wooded terrain to the perimeter of El Gori's secluded hideo-ut.

The plan was for them to scale the eight-foot concrete fence sur-rounding the house from the rear and make entry, while Gori and his cohorts were sound asleep. But no plan is perfect, and sometimes one must adjust on the fly. The marines did not expect for Gori and his cohorts to still be partying and living it up at four in the morning, music blaring at ear-splitting levels, but they were. We later learned that Gori's second in command and new plaza boss of Monterrey, known as "El Flaco" was celebrating his recent promotion at the Quinta with Gori and his boys and getting a jump start on the upcoming Lupe-Reyes celebration.

The team had no choice but to wait them out.

The unforeseen delay worked to our advantage, providing the team a chance to recuperate from the long trek and regain some much-needed energy, while Gori, Flaco and his boys whooped it up and got drunker by the minute. The downside was that sunrise would be upon us shortly and we would lose the cover of darkness. But at least our guys were sober, alert and well rested. The thick woods provided excellent cover in the darkness of the wintry dawn. For the moment, we held the tactical advantage and still had the element of surprise in our favor. We decided to let them party themselves out—a tactical Rope-a-Dope strategy, like what Ali used on Foreman in their famous Rumble in the Jungle fight in Zaire. By the time Gori and his boys were done, they would be incapacitated and totally outmatched, just like Foreman.

Unfazed by the biting chilly mountain air, the blaring music went on well after sunrise. The team, hidden in the wooded thicket behind the Quinta, patiently endured the frigid temperature and waited till the last sounds of party life drifted away into the icy mist and the clouds enshrouding the Cerro de La Silla. The radiant morning sun provided a brief respite from the biting cold as the team checked each other's equipment for one last time before showtime. Adrenaline was pumping, but an air of self-composure and confidence prevailed among the team as they approached the concrete fence behind the Quinta.

The lead member of the team employed the tactical ladder, and the first team member swiftly scaled it. Upon reaching the top, he pulled out a large hammer from his belt and smashed the razor-sharp glass shards embedded in the concrete to deter burglars. Burglars, not highly trained military operatives. Smoothly and rapidly, each member crossed the fence and onto Gori's property. They slowly made their way to the house and split up, sending a team of five to the front of the house as three remained in the back to cover the back door. The team slowly snaked its way from the north side of the house to affect the east-facing entry from the front. As they turned the corner to approach the east wall, a member of Goris' team turned the corner and almost ran right into the first team member. His mouth dropped wide open as he stared in disbelief before turning and running towards the front door screaming, "Wachos! Aqui estan los Wachos!" (Soldiers! The soldiers are here!)

The team remained calm and proceeded slowly and methodically towards the front door. The runner stopped suddenly at the front door, pulled a handgun from under his shirt and started firing at the team and warning his fellow Zetas. It was his last action before a marine bullet pierced his skull.

All hell broke loose.

Shots scattered indiscriminately as the Zetas scrambled to escape or take cover. Like roaches hiding from bright lights, they ran out of the house in droves from the front and back doors, firing shots randomly. They were no match for the highly trained marines who wasted no bullets on indiscriminate shots. Blood-curdling screams of desperation and agony from the wounded, and those trying to escape, pierced the stillness of the crisp mountain morning. Some Zetas started up a gray Chevy Suburban and hauled ass out of there, breaking down the driveway gate in the process and tearing out of the range of marine fire. The marine team leader called out the description of the Suburban to the approaching reinforcement team so they could be on the lookout in case Gori had escaped in the van.

After what seemed like an eternity, the shooting stopped. The smell of blood and gunpowder commingled with the fresh mountain air as the team secured the prisoners—nine in total—and processed the carnage at the scene. It was nothing short of surreal. It felt as though one had been thrust into the middle of a Stephen King horror story. Pools of blood, fragments of skull and clumps of brain matter seemed to be everywhere. The marines rounded up the prisoners in the backyard, securing their hands with zip ties and covering their heads with jackets or shirts to prevent them from identifying any of the marines' faces. They had been so surprised that they had not even put their pants on when the operation went down. The prisoners huddled together in the backyard, shivering in their skivvies and biting cold, literally freezing their asses off.

We anxiously awaited the word that Gori was either in custody or killed. Inside the compound, the team leader stared into the lifeless eyes of the once feared Gori—who ironically died in his underwear with an expression of disbelief and horror on his face—and then called to confirm that they had eliminated him. After all the smoke had cleared, eight Zetas lost their lives at the Quinta that morning, including Gori and El Flaco—two birds with one stone. We could not have asked for a better scenario. And, the shootout did not injure a single Marine.

But the day was not over yet.

The gray Suburban rumbled down the back roads of Colonia Bosques de la Silla, leaving a tornado of dust in its wake. They were desperately trying to reach the main thoroughfare so they could blend into the mainstream traffic and get away clean.

"What do we do if we run into more of them? We cannot outrun them in this piece of shit!" said the passenger.

"Shut your mouth! Don't be a pussy ass bitch and get ready to fight it out with them if we do see them again!" barked the driver known as "El Gonzo."

El Gonzo was the senior Zeta on the scene and by default took charge of the small group of seven Zetas that had escaped the marine operation at the Quinta, along with two kidnap victims who had spent the night handcuffed in the back of the truck. Holding to their demented nicknaming conventions, the Zetas named him Gonzo because he had droopy eyes and a long-curved hook nose, which looked much like the Sesame Street Muppet.

Someone over at the Zeta HR nickname department had a warped and deranged sense of humor. Gonzo vowed not to be taken alive. Not that escaping would be much better for him. If he were to escape with his life, Miguel Trevino would take care of ensuring he suffered a worse and more painful death than the comrades he had left behind at the Quinta. The two kidnap victims they had in the back of the van were crying and pleading to be let out of the vehicle, but Gonzo did not care. He kept the pedal to the metal, determined to make it to the main road. Those whiny bastards had been kidnapped because they claimed to be Zetas and were extorting people on the streets, so he didn't give two fucks about those whiny mopes. They weren't whining when they received huge amounts of extortion money that rightfully belonged to the Zetas, not them. They weren't whining when they spent all the extortion money drinking bottle after bottle of Don Julio Tequila or banging the best-looking whores in Monterrey. As far as Gonzo was concerned, whatever their fate, they deserved it. No, Gonzo didn't feel one ounce of pity for these ass wipes. They wanted to be Zetas? Well, now they had a front-row seat on the ride, as to what real Zeta life was like, even if that ride went straight to hell.

Gonzo had already reached out for reinforcements the minute they left the Quinta. The reinforcements would wait for them near the main road where they could then take the highway to Reynosa and lie low until things settled down.

He would figure out what to do with the whiners later.

Although it was a chilly day, sweat ran down Gonzo's temples and forehead. He shut out the whimpering noises coming from the kidnap victims and rambled on. He could already see the traffic running up and down the main road, but he did not expect that other people were ahead of him, also trying to get access to the Reynosa highway. The traffic backed up almost thirty yards to the main intersection. Eight trucks packed with Zeta reinforcements were waiting for them at the intersection and Gonzo was not going to sit patiently in traffic to await his turn.

"Fuck it! Agarrense cabrones!" (Hold on assholes!)

He violently pulled off the northbound lane, jumped the curb, tires squealing and smoking, and crossed over into the southbound lane against traffic. "I have to make it!" he muttered under his breath and plowed onward, straight into the path of the oncoming marine reinforcement team.

"A la verga!! Los Wachos disparen cabrones disparen!!" (Holy fuck! The soldiers! Shoot assholes! Shoot!)

Gonzo practically plowed the vehicle into the military truck, narrowly missing it as his passenger fired blindly at the oncoming military vehicles, jump starting the second shootout of the day with the marines. A blinding volley of heavy gunfire met them as Gonzo's passengers exited the Suburban and engaged the marines with reckless abandon. Gonzo fired his AK-47 through the windshield of the minivan, hoping that he could provide enough cover so he could try to get away and leave with the Zeta reinforcements. He adjusted and

jumped to the empty passenger side seat to get a better shooting angl
e.

Time seemed to stand still for Gonzo as he put hot lead down range, when he suddenly saw movement from the corner of his eye and turned to see the source of the movement—a lone marine in a crouching stance sighting a grenade launcher in his direction. He saw the marine's lips move, but there is no way he could have heard the words "Fuego!" (Fire in the hole!) Then a loud thump.

The last thing Gonzo would ever see was the 40mm round leaving the barrel of the M203 grenade launcher, blazing a trail of smoke right towards him before everything went dark for Gonzo's world.

Boom!

The force of the deafening explosion lifted the van into the air, shattered the windows of surrounding vehicles and left the remaining Zetas shell shocked, and scattering for cover. Flames engulfed the Suburban, burning Gonzo and the kidnap victims beyond recognition.

Chaos erupted in apocalyptic proportions. Black smoke billowed into the sky from the smoldering flames. Christmas decorations dangled precariously after being destroyed by incoming gunfire. Inflated snowmen and Santa Clauses were not immune to the destruction, as high caliber bullets pierced their plastic skin. Innocent bystanders screamed, terror-stricken, as they ran for cover under the torrential rain of gunfire. Vendors selling fruits and vegetables huddled under their makeshift stands, reciting the Hail Mary repeatedly and hoping to survive to see the end of the day.

The Zetas and their reinforcements were no match for the heavy artillery used by the marines. A second explosion delivered from the M203 convinced the Zetas that it was time to hightail it out of there and live to fight another day. But the fleeing Zetas left behind a group of their comrades to fend for themselves. Some of them commandeered a taxi and sped away, leaving a several members behind. The final Zetas wisely surrendered. When it finally ended, the authorities arrested seven Zetas at the scene. Four more were dead, including Gonzo, the two kidnap victims, and one unidentified Zeta. Unfortunately, the Zetas killed an innocent bystander with a stray round from their erratic, undisciplined, and haphazard shooting.

We eliminated twelve Zetas that day, including two significant Zeta leaders in Gori and El Flaco. We arrested sixteen more, bringing the total number of Zetas removed from the equation in one day to twenty-eight. The Marines also took 36 firearms along with 11 grenades and 13 vehicles off the streets. The Marines made their presence known. Our intelligence would reveal that this operation left the Zetas reeling in confusion and bewilderment.

Miguel Trevino found himself grappling with a formidable new force in SEMAR, leaving him unsure of how to navigate the situation. It felt satisfying to know that the tables had turned. Trevino was now fearful for his fate. Our intelligence revealed that he basically went underground after this operation and took extreme measures of security. Our determination grew as we narrowed the gap between us and him, and we couldn't afford to lose momentum. This operation definitely proved to be a turning point for the war on organized crime in Mexico because of SEMARS proficiency and attention to detail in their operational planning. Two weeks later, the SEMAR team carried out another operation in Cuernavaca, Morelos. They successfully eliminated Arturo Beltran Leyva, also known as "El jefe de los jefes" (Boss of bosses), and five of his associates amidst a fierce exchange of gunfire. Images of a deceased Arturo Beltran Leyva, resembling Swiss cheese, with stacks of dollar bills on his lifeless body were leaked to the media. It was a subtle message to all criminals. No amount of money was going to buy your way out of the inevitable. For all the bad shit you do and all the bad shit you have done to innocent people, don't fear the reaper when he comes knocking on your door, for you will hear him knocking eventually.

Just ask Gori, Flaco, Gonzo, and the former Jefe de jefes - they all have the answers.

SEMAR troops run for cover during shootout with El Gori's crew.
(Photo courtesy of Grupo Reforma / El Norte)

Chapter 14: 2011 Agents Down

2011 will forever be etched in our memories as a year of both profound tragedy and unforgettable moments. If there was one year that I could go back in time and erase from existence, it would be this one. I never believed things could get worse than they already were, but unbelievably they did. The events that unfolded that year took a heavy toll on the human spirit, mind, and soul. With over 2000 homicides, 139 of which were innocent victims, 2011 went down as the most violent year in the history of Nuevo Leon and was one of the first years I ever recall questioning my faith. It was without a doubt one of the most stressful and difficult years of my life. The whole year was a blur to me. I know many of my DEA counterparts have been through many stressful times, but I would bet money that what we as a team went through that entire year, would rank right up there with the toughest of times anywhere, anytime.

The reality of being an agent in a foreign country is often far from the glamorous and action-packed scenes depicted in movies. The movies often neglect to show the reality that sometimes there is tedious and unpleasant work that cannot be avoided. We all get our share of shit work, especially if you are a supervisor. During the week of February 13, 2011, I was up to my ears in shit work, as I was preparing our office for our yearly inspection. If I was going to be up to my ears in shit work, my staff was going to be deep in it as well. I was certainly not going to drown in shit all by myself. In a US Consulate, Federal Law Enforcement agencies are represented by a small staff of agents and administrative personnel. ICE, FBI, ATF and USCIS each have thei r own offices, and each has its own list of shit work to do occasionally. This week, aside from our office, ICE agents Victor Avila and Jaime Zapata were given a major shit assignment. They were to drive from their assigned post in Mexico City to San Luis Potosi, pick up some important equipment from ICE agents assigned to Monterrey, and promptly return to Mexico City—a total round trip of ten hours driving, not counting stops for restroom breaks, or refueling, for possibly twelve hours on the road. Normally a road trip like this would be a pleasant respite from being cooped up in the office all day, but in 2010, the State department issued a travel warning to all US Citizens, Embassy, and Consulate employees because of the dangerous environment created by the war between the Zetas and t he Gulf Cartel.

The travel warning specifically stated that:

'Effective July 15,2010, Mission employees may not travel by vehicle across the US-Mexico border to or from any post in Mexico.' The warning also states that 'criminals appear to especially target SUVS and full-size pick-up trucks for theft and carjacking.'

Ironically, these are just the kind of vehicles US Law Enforcement employees drive—fully armored Chevy Suburbans, Toyota Landcruisers, or Ford Expeditions, also the preferred vehicles of drug traffickers.

Victor Avila, from the outset, had a bad feeling about this assignment, and he addressed the issue with his boss. Whatever piece of equipment that needed to be picked up was important enough to risk the safety of two agents in Mexico City and two agents from Monterrey. These agents had to travel to Laredo, Texas, pick up the valuable equipment and deliver it to Victor and Jaime in San Luis Potosi, all in a blatant violation of the State Department Travel restriction. Our agents in Monterrey were not allowed to drive to the border, which was only a two-hour drive. However, Jaime and Victor were instructed to take a twelve-hour road trip in territory that was well documented as being dangerous, all for an unspecified piece of equipment. It just made little sense at all. The worst part of ICE management's plan was that no other agency knew about the trip. At least the DEA Monterrey did not. Our ICE counterparts did not tell us at all.

So, on February 15, 2011, I focused on finalizing preparations for the upcoming yearly office inspection. Shit work, lots of it. But it was imperative that I finish it. I had no clue that ICE agents from Mexico City were traveling into San Luis Potosi, our area of responsibility. Nor did I know Monterrey ICE agents were also in San Luis Potosi to deliver the alleged important piece of equipment.

I was completely oblivious to the tsunami of a shit storm that was about to rock our worlds.

Earlier that morning, Victor Avila and Jaime Zapata left the bubble of the US Embassy and the swarming turbulence that was Mexico City. The streets were unusually quiet at 5 am as they headed north towards San Luis Potosi. Neither agent knew the other, up until the previous day, but they hit it off as though they had been friends for a lifetime. They said nothing as they took Highway 57 north, each sipping his Starbucks coffee as the radio blared some mundane narco-corrido, a ballad glorifying the lives of narco traffickers. It seemed that was the only music played on radio stations now a days. Knowing it would be a long trip, both opted to enjoy the silence for now, in a sort of meditative state. There would be plenty to talk about later. Jaime used this time to say a silent prayer for the success of the mission, and asked God to take care of his parents, his brothers, his fiancé, the rest of his family. He finally asked for a quick and safe return for him and Victor.

He made the sign of the cross, took a sip of his coffee and asked, "So how was your Valentine's Day bro?"

"It was quiet bro, we didn't really do much because of this trip, you know? Having to get up early and all. Doesn't give you many options. Me and the wife had a quiet dinner and went to bed early. How about you?"

"Same here. Just stayed in the hotel and talked to my girlfriend on the phone. Didn't want to be a fuck up and wake up late for this assignment." He snickered as he said it.

Victor nodded with a smile and said, "Yeah, it sucks. But what are you going to do? Gotta just suck it up, right?"

"No shit."

"So, what do you think of Mexico City so far? Having any fun out here?"

"For the short time I have been here, I really like it so far. I wouldn't mind working out here permanently. It is completely different from what I am used to."

"Well, take advantage of the face time you get with the brass while you are here on assignment, bro. Once they get to know you and you do your job well, you may get an inside track on getting a permanent slot here in Mexico City bro."

"We shall see. There are a lot of things I have to consider before I make a life-changing decision like that, bro."

"It is a big decision! But you have to weigh the pros and the cons. If you get selected for a spot up here, the G pays for your housing and utilities. Stuff like cable and internet are on you but that is cheap. We also get danger pay up here! So, there are many perks that are to your advantage. Career wise, you will mingle with high-ranking people from all federal agencies based in Mexico City that may help you advance your career. Just saying dude so you can keep that in mind if you make your decision. Beats the hell out of Laredo, Texas bro."

Jaime stayed deep in thought, contemplating Victor's advice, looking out the window of the armored Suburban as the sprawling urban landscape gave way to the cactus lined Mexican countryside. He wondered what life would be like if he transferred to one of the largest cities in the world. This was the major leagues for a law enforcement agent. The possibilities were endless. But would his fiancé be happy? What about his parents? They were getting on in age and he would not be as accessible as he would be in the United States. There were so many factors to consider.

"Hey Victor. Let me ask you something."

"Sure anything bro. What's up?"

"If I should decide to transfer and actually get assigned here, can I somehow watch the Dallas Cowboys games here during the season?" Do you all have cable TV up here?"

Victor, an avid Cowboys fan himself, broke into a hearty laugh and looked at Jaime who was solemnly staring at him dead serious, worried about Victor's answer.

"Yeah man! You can watch any NFL game you want down here. This is not a third world country, bro! We have cable TV, and we even have a group of Cowboys fans here that get together to barbecue and watch the games occasionally. It's all good." He chuckled as he held out his fist to fist bump Jaime.

"You're going to be alright brother." They both shared a long laugh.

As soon as Victor mentioned barbecue, Jaime went into a long discourse about his love for the grill and the myriad of smoking techniques used for preparing beef brisket, beef ribs, pork ribs, venison, turkey, chicken, fish, and sausage for the best dining experience one could ever have. He spoke excitedly about the countless family traditions spent around a smoking grill in Brownsville, Texas, his passion for hunting white-tailed deer and feral hogs in the mesquite rich ranches of Starr County and his love for saltwater fishing along the many inlets of the Laguna Madre and the tremendous but rewarding challenge of big game fishing in the deep blue waters of the Gulf of Mexico. The down-to-earth quality of the conversation made the long drive to San Luis Potosi less tedious to both agents. Time seemed to evaporate with the conversation, even though they made a couple of pit stops along the way to refuel and for bathroom breaks.

Victor developed a genuine respect for the younger agent he had just met 24 hours earlier and vowed to help him in any way he could whether he transferred to Mexico City in the future or not. The trip provided a pathway to an unbreakable bond of brotherhood that many Law Enforcement officers develop during missions and extended time together. They arrived in San Luis Potosi at approximately 11:30 am, hungry and tired of sitting down.

They met up with the Monterrey agents at a famous truck stop known as "Parador El Potosino," and loaded 12 boxes containing the valuable equipment into their vehicle. The agents from both offices exchanged pleasantries and went their separate ways.

"I don't know about you, bro, but I am starving. I could use a big ass subway right about now," said Jaime, pointing to the Subway's sign. He was still used to the United States timetable, which meant eating lunch at noon. In Mexico, lunch begins at 2 PM and typically lasts until 4 PM.

"I could use some chow brother, let's go inside and check it out."

Parador El Potosino holds bragging rights as the largest truck stop in the entire Republic of Mexico. A sprawling one stop shopping center that hosts hundreds of thousands of travelers on a yearly basis. Weary travelers can whet their appetites from an array of restaurants inside the shopping center, from typical regional Mexican cuisine to Church's Fried Chicken, Subway, Papa John's Pizza, to flavorful yogurt and ice cream shops. There is a play area for restless children, a lounge area with comfortable couches, where one can sit and watch television or just relax and take a quick nap, a billiard room, a gym with several treadmills, stationary bikes and weights, a large convenience store that sells every type of snack or cold beverage one can imagine, including artisanal curios, typical of San Luis Potosi. This 60,000 square foot monstrosity stands smack in the middle of the San Luis Potosi desert land surrounded by agave cacti, prickly pear cacti, yucca palms blooming bunches of pearly white flowers and the Potosino mountainside where red-tailed hawks, prairie falcons and Golden eagles float among the clouds, roaming the desert for possum, armadillos, rabbits, prairie dogs and squirrels. However, hawks, falcons and eagles aren't the only ones searching for prey amongst the Potosino desert.

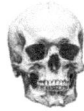

The Zetas have nicknames for everyone. Like Gonzo, they sometimes use these nicknames to comically reference a specific physical defect in someone. With "La Mosca" (The fly), two physical defects were the rationale behind his Zeta moniker. He was a very small man with enormous round eyes, like the headlights on a vintage Volkswagen beetle. They never took him seriously because of his size, about 4 feet and eight inches, and never accepted him as a true member of the Zetas.

His assignment was to hang out at El Potosino and report any suspicious activity that he observed. For this, he received a paltry sum of four hundred pesos per week. The equivalent of twenty US dollars, barely enough to get by. He yearned to win the favor of his bosses so he could one day be a respected member of the fearful Zetas, earn wads of money, drive expensive vehicles, and win the adoration of beautiful women. Seeking a transformation of his impoverished and unfortunate life, he constantly prayed to the Santa Muerte. He usually hung around the gas pumps, panhandling, and hoping to earn enough to buy something to eat or drink later. He had just scored twenty pesos off a family at the pumps and was on his way to the store when he saw the shiny blue Chevy Suburban pull up in front of the Subway restaurant. Two well-dressed men got out of the vehicle and walked inside. They spoke in a language he did not understand and had never heard before. Their vehicle had license plates with blue lettering that he had never seen before. He hid behind the vehicle along the passenger side and knocked on the window. It was solid as granite on a frigid winter day. He knew enough about these vehicles to deduce that it was an armored vehicle. A vehicle not usually seen around the streets of San Luis except for the ones driven by his bosses. Could it be that the huesudita, (Santa Muerte), had finally answered his prayers? He excitedly scampered off into the shadows of the immense truck stop, pulled out his Nextel, and call ed his boss.

El Piolin had called it a night at 5 AM on the morning of February 15. He had been on all night bender since 2 PM the previous day, Valentine's Day. Unfortunately, Piolin did not have a true Valentine. He used his position as the leader of a Zeta estaca (6 to 8 member team) to force any girl he desired to be his Valentine on February 14—or any other day, for that matter—if he so wished. Be my Valentine or die bitch was his mindset, every day, every month, every year. With nothing more than a grade three education, all Piolon had ever known was violence. In his mind, might meant right, and with cocaine and alcohol constantly flowing through his veins his level of violence caught the attention of high-ranking Zeta leader and Plaza Boss for San Luis Potosi, Jesus Rejon aka "El Mamito", who made him an estaca leader.

Today he was in a foul mood, nursing a monstrous hangover, and had no patience to take a call from "La Mosca." He handed the phone to one of his men, a guy known as, "El Safado" (The looney one).

"Aver que quiere este pendejo!" (See what this dumbass wants).

El Safado took the phone and answered.

"Que chingados quieres pinche Mosca? Siempre molestando!" (What the fuck do you want fucking Mosca? Always bothering people!).

"Dile al jefe que hay algo raro por aqui!" (Tell the boss there is something weird out here!)

"Pos explicate pendejo!! Dejate de chingaderas!" (Well, explain yourself dumbass and stop fucking around.)

"Hay dos bueyes que no son de aqui! Estan en una camioneta blindada Con placas muy raras! (There are two guys that are not from here. They are in an armored vehicle with weird license plates.)

El Safado looked at Piolin and repeated the information provided by La Mosca.

"Where are they now?" barked Piolin.

"Donde estan ahorita pendejo!" (Where are they now dumbass?)

Excited by the opportunity and the significance of what it could mean for his future, the pitch of La Mosca's voice rose in a comical falsetto tone.

"Ya se van! Ya se van!" (They are leaving! They are leaving!)

He screamed frantically into the phone, jumping up and down excitedly as the Chevy Suburban left the parking lot of El Parador Potosino and merged into the flowing traffic on Highway 57 bound for Mexico City.

"Dice que ya se van! Se subieron a la Carretera rumbo a La Capirucha!!" (He said that they left on the highway heading towards the Capitol.)

"Dile a todo el equipo que busquen a estos cabrones sobre la carretera! Diles que vamos en camino!" (Tell the rest of the team to look for these assholes on the highway and that we are enroute!)

El Safado focused on the road and floored the gas pedal in search of the unsuspecting ICE agents, who were eager to get back to normality in their comfort zone in Mexico City.

Jaime volunteered to drive the suburban back to Mexico City, feeling that he had to contribute other than just a being a tag along. He had never driven an armored vehicle in his life and was anxious to get the feel of what it would be like to drive one of these monsters. Victor welcomed the relief, and he used the break to call his supervisor and brief him on their status. He advised that they had received the equipment and were heading back to Mexico City, probably arriving around 6 PM. Just in time for rush hour, thought Victor.

They had been on the road for about an hour when Jaime noticed two vehicles behind them, closing in fast on their Suburban. He couldn't help but notice the barrel of a long gun sticking out of the rear window of the driver's side. His heart started pounding.

"We have company, bro! There is a long gun sticking out of the back seat window. Do you see it?"

Victor turned around to get a good look at the vehicles behind them and immediately noticed that the vehicles were fully occupied by armed individuals. His heart dropped to his knees as he immediately turned around and shouted to Jaime, "Whatever you do, do not stop! Keep going!"

Adrenaline jacked up to the sky. Jaime floored it. But the weight of the armored suburban was too much of a load for the engine, that reluctantly responded as Piolin's team of hit men closed in on them.

"Esos son! Ya los temenos alcanzalos pendejo," yelled Piolin at El Safado. (That's them! We have them! Catch up to them, asshole!)

Safado stepped on the gas and easily overtook the much heavier Suburban.

Fucking Mosca finally did something right, he thought to himself. Everyone locked and loaded, adrenaline coming out of their ears as they pulled alongside the vehicle. Everyone started shouting at once to the strangers in the blue suburban.

"Ahorinse cabrones! Ahorinse hijos de su puta madre!" (Pull over! Pull over motherfuckers!)

"Do not stop bro! Keep going!" shouted Victor.

They were both paralyzed with angst and fear as the most terrifyingly horrid dream materialized right before their eyes. One vehicle raced swiftly ahead of them, swerved to the right, and stopped directly in front of their suburban. The second vehicle came to a screeching halt directly behind them, effectively boxing them in. Jaime, feeling he had no choice, put the vehicle in park. Victor counted at least eight heavily armed gunmen pour out of their vehicles, yelling obscenities and pointing their weapons directly at him and Jaime.

The situation was surreal. Everything seemed to slow down as the gunmen yelled at them to get out of the vehicle. One of them came over to the driver's side door and yanked it open. It's amazing how we take minor details for granted until they are not minor details anymore. When Jaime put the vehicle in park, the doors automatically unlocked, a feature that is standard in all GMC vehicles. Jaime struggled with the gunman to get the door closed again and pulled as hard as he could. Finally, closing it and hanging on for dear life as the gunman tried to pry open the door.

"Lock the doors! Lock the doors!" he shouted desperately.

Victor frantically searched for the door lock button and inadvertently hit the window button. The passenger side window automatically rolled down about two inches. Two gunmen immediately took advantage of this development and introduced their weapons into the vehicle. Victor recognized the weapons as an AK-47 and a .45 caliber handgun, both of which were inches from his face.

"We are American diplomats from the US Embassy!"

Victor shouted at the gunmen. He may as well have been talking Chinese because no one among them spoke English or had the faintest idea of what a diplomat was. They were out for blood. The look in their collective eyes projected pure homicidal evil. It was the most fear either agent had ever experienced in their lives. Victor leaned back in his seat as he anxiously searched for the window button.

"We are diplomats! This is a diplomatic vehicle!" He pleaded helplessly!

He looked straight into the eyes of El Piolin as he gave the order to shoot.

"Acabenlos a esos cabrones!" (Finish off those assholes!)

El Safado smiled as he and his cohort pulled the trigger on the strangers who dared to invade their territory.

The thunderous roar of the weapons shattered their eardrums as Victor miraculously found the window button and clicked it. The gunman had removed their weapons from within the vehicle just as the window rolled up. But it was too late. Victor was hit, but Jaime got the worst of it. Gunsmoke permeated the cabin of their vehicles as they both cried out in pain.

"Estan vivos todavia pendejos! Matenlos ya!" (They are still alive you idiots! Finish them off now!) Barked Piolin to the rest of the group. They did as ordered and fired off a volley of gunfire at the vehicle.

"I'm hit! I'm hit!" cried Jaime in agony.

"Take off, let's go!! Let's get out of here!"

"I'm going to die bro! I'm going to die!"

"Listen to me! You will not die! You hear me? Now let's get the fuck out of here!" shouted Victor.

Jaime was unresponsive and fading fast. Blood spewed forth from his femoral artery as his head slowly lilted to one side. Out of the corner of his eye, Victor saw the vehicles of the gunman take off, speeding down the highway. He was helpless to do anything to stop Jaime from bleeding. In pain himself from his three wounds, one to the leg, the arm and another to his midsection, he knew he had to take quick action if there was any way, they were going to survive.

With his left hand, he jerked the gearshift into drive and leaned over and pushed Jaime's leg onto the gas pedal, but the Suburban's engine had also suffered severe damage and had no power. The vehicle slowly rolled along the highway, coming to a stop on the median. Luck seemed to have slipped away and gone into hiding that day, because just as the truck came to a halt, Victor spotted Piolin's hit team returning to the scene.

Jaime was already unconscious. A human could bleed out within minutes of a serious femoral artery injury, and Victor fumbled around the cabin in search of his phone to call for help. Everything happened so fast that he did not know where the phone had gone. His hands were trembling as he watched the hit team speeding closer and closer to his vehicle. He had to get a message to the Embassy before they finished him and Jaime off.

As the hit team approach and pulled up in front of their vehicle, his heart rate raced and his breath came up short. He couldn't find the phone anywhere. Luck was not handing out any favors that day, especially for them. He watched what he considered were the last moments of his life, as two gunmen emerged from the vehicle. They locked eyes as they trained their weapons on the front windshield of the suburban and opened fire.

"Please God, take care of my family!" he cried out, closing his eyes, as the bullets shattered the silence and the suburban's windshield.

After a few seconds, Victor opened his eyes. The armored suburban had done its job and prevented the rounds from penetrating the windshield. As the smoke cleared, the assailants got back in their vehicle and sped away. Victor fought off the overwhelming shock caused by the chaos and found his blackberry phone. He then called th e office of the Regional Security office at the Embassy and frantically explained that he and Jaime had been ambushed and shot. He made his next call to one of his most trusted contacts, a high-ranking commander of the Federal Police, and explained again that he and Jaime had been ambushed on the highway, were critically wounded, and desperately needed backup. Approximately forty minutes after the call to the commander, a Federal Police Blackhawk helicopter landed

on the highway and took both agents to the hospital in San Luis Potosi
.

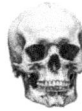

I was on my lunch break when I got the call from the Regional Security officer. Whenever he called, I knew something had to be wrong. My blood froze in my veins as I answered the call. He explained to me, out of breath, that two ICE agents had been shot in San Luis Potosi and instructed me to return to the Consulate immediately for an Emergency Action meeting. I left my lunch on the table, ran out the door and hauled ass to the Consulate. Adrenaline raced through my veins as I swerved in and out of the lunchtime traffic to reach the Consulate. All Law Enforcement personnel gathered in the Consul general's conference room, and I joined them to receive a briefing on what had happened. One Monterrey ICE agent was present at the meeting, and he briefed us on what he knew. He was clearly rattled and emotional.

"This afternoon at approximately 2 PM, two of our agents from Mexico City were ambushed on Highway 57 in San Luis Potosi. One agent is deceased, and the other agent is critically wounded and in the hospital in San Luis Potosi. They were apparently ambushed on the road by several gunmen, whom we believe to be the Zetas, because we all know that they control that corridor. We do not know what the motive may have been. Federal Police are on the scene and are reporting developments as needed."

The room was silent. We had no words to describe our sentiments. Another tragedy had befallen us and another one of our fellow law enforcement agents was gone. But we really had no time to lament his passing. There was an agent in a hospital in San Luis Potosi who needed immediate attention, not in a Mexican hospital, but in a United States hospital.

The RSO took over the meeting and said that he and his assistant were going to provide support in San Luis Potosi and needed volunteers for the trip. It was a tense moment. Everyone wanted to go, but we could not all go. The Monterrey ICE agent had been instructed by his superiors in Monterrey to stay in Monterrey and not take part in the support response. Myself and the most senior agent on my staff were to stay behind to take care of the incoming inspection team. The decision was made for the RSO, his assistant, two of my agents, and one FBI agent to go on the trip to San Luis Potosi. If I had my way, all of us would have gone to assist in whatever way we could, but somebody had to stay behind.

Darkness and night had befallen the city of San Luis Potosi by the time our team arrived. The streets were eerily quiet, which enhanced the intensity of the team's mission. I had assigned two highly experienced agents, Stan Hartman and Fred Gomez, to make the trip and brief me every step of the way. When I spoke to Hartman later that night, he described in great detail their welcome to the State of San L uis.

As they got there, they noticed a swarm of Federal Police milling around the exterior of the Hospital, shooting the shit and laughing it up as if they were at a backyard barbeque or party. They immediately entered the hospital and were met by one of the Federal police commanders, who introduced himself to our RSO, Mark Mitchel. After the cursory introductions, he told Mitchel that for safety purposes they would have to search all bags before letting them in to see Victor Avila. There was absolutely no way they were going to let him or his subordinates to search their respective bags and Mitchel strongly made the point that they were all under diplomatic protection and any such request had to be made to and approved by the US Ambassador. The commander backed off and explained to Mitchel that he was only following orders. The agents certainly did not want the Federal Police locating weapons, which they weren't supposed to have in the first place and making what was already a terrible situation eve n worse."

The priority was to assist Victor in any way they could, in the best way that they could. The commander gave them Victor's room number, cursory directions on getting there, and disappeared into the darkness. The hallways were dimly lit accompanied by an eerie silence which is highly uncommon in most hospitals. The phone at the nurse's station was ringing incessantly as they approached Victor's room. The only other audible sound was the sound of their footsteps clanking and echoing on the hospital floor.

"They expected to see Federal police standing guard outside Victor's room, but there was no one to be found, anywhere. Victor was alone in the room, terrified and traumatized by the shooting. He adamantly refused the administration of any painkillers and was running on pure adrenalin. The scene was similar to the scene in the Godfather when all of Don Corleone's bodyguards had been sent away, leaving Don Corleone alone in his room. Hartman told Victor that they were with DEA out of the US Consulate in Monterrey and were there to protect him and exfiltrate him back to safety in the United States. The only way to accomplish that was with a DEA air craft."

After speaking to Hartman, many heated calls between our office and the US Embassy took place, bickering about the numerous excuses why our aircraft, a DEA aircraft, could not be sent immediately. Excuses ranging from the hangar and the control tower being closed to no one being available to open up the Fixed Base Operator (FBO), or man the tower—all bull shit excuses.

On a conference call with my bosses in Mexico and Ambassador Carlos Pascual listening in, I expressed my frustration with the situation and reminded them of the time Juan Garcia Abrego sent a hit team to a hospital in an attempt to finish off a rival. The Zetas have a clean-up crew that comes to crime scenes to finish victims that survive an attack. They have many people on their payroll, possibly even people who can grant easy access to the hospital. I said this situation is urgent! We already have one agent dead boss; I do not want to be responsible for the death of another one, knowing we could have done something. Call whoever you have to call in the Mexican Government to get the damn tower in operation and let's get Victor out of there ASAP before the Zetas come back to finish him.

I don't know who called who, but within the hour, the FBO was opened up and several air traffic controllers showed up to get our plane wheels up and off to San Luis Potosi. At approximately 0300, they removed Victor from the hospital, with literally only the hospital gown he was wearing, took him to the airport, loaded him into the DEA aircraft, and safely flew him to Houston Texas where his life, those of his family members and Zapata's family would never be the same. Victor's family was evacuated from Mexico City immediately after the shooting. They took only a suitcase of basic necessities, leaving everything they owned, even the coffeemaker, at their residence in Mexico City. All Victor had by way of clothes was the hospital gown he was given in Mexico. Hell, he didn't even have a toothbrush. They reunited in Houston, Texas and had to restart their lives from scratch, while dealing with the trauma from the incide nt.

It took a coordinated and persistently intense effort between DEA, FBI, US Marshalls, CIA and SEMAR for approximately a month of tireless work and sleepless nights to capture El Piolin and others associated with Zapata's murder, and the near murder of Avila. Our intelligence indicated that Miguel Trevino was furious at the entire crew of the San Luis Plaza and ordered the Regional Plaza Boss Jesus Rejon Aguilar, aka "El Mamito" aka "Z-7", to turn himself in to authorities or face the execution of his entire family, women, and children included. The last thing Trevino wanted was more heat from the United States government and the decisions made by El Mamito's crew brought an inferno of heat not seen since DEA agent Enrique Camarena's kidnapping in 1985. El Mamito, a former Special Forces operative and founding member of the Zetas, was highly respected among his peers. This mattered little to Trevino in these circumstances, and he wanted El Mamito either dead or in jail.

Shortly after the shooting, "El Mamito" went into hiding in Mexico City, but when your country's entire armed forces and a ruthlessly vicious cartel boss are hunting you down, you can't hide for very long. The Federal police captured El Mamito in Mexico City in July 2011, without one shot being fired. The authorities extradited him to the United States in September 2012 to face drug trafficking charges. He entered a guilty plea and is now facing a maximum sentence of life in prison. La Mosca was never seen or heard from again. It is rumored that he was burned alive in the loneliness of the desert of San Luis Potosi, for providing false information to the Zeta leadership.

The lives of many families changed on that fateful day in 2011. No matter how many Zeta members we arrested, Jaime Zapata was never coming back. Victor Avila would forever bear the trauma inflicted upon him by the attack and the subsequent death of Jaime. But what could have offered some consolation were answers to several questions that to this day have not been addressed. What piece of equipment was so important that called for the unnecessary risk of several agents' lives? That risk ended up costing the life of a promising young agent who was just getting stared in life.

At the time, Victor's boss advised that the special item that needed to be picked up was an important piece of equipment, necessary for the enhancement of ICE's mission in Mexico. If that was the case, then why were the contents in Victor and Jaime's suburban packed to the gills with cardboard boxes, if it was only one piece of equipment? All this for one piece of equipment? I have seen a lot of equipment used in investigations. And, in all my 28 years of law enforcement have never seen a piece of equipment that would require being packaged in so many cardboard boxes to fill up an entire suburban. Why is there no mention anywhere of the contents inside those cardboard boxes? Why is there no inventory of the items recovered from the bullet riddled suburban? Who has this information? The FBI, ICE? DEA certainly does not have it. The priority of the DEA was to extract Victor safely from the hospital and locate the Zeta members responsible for the attack.

Another point to consider is that DEA aircraft regularly make several trips to the United States border from Mexico City. Surely, they could have planned a special trip for what was deemed "special equipment" and utilized the aircraft to pick up and deliver the "special equipment" with no risk to agents in the field. Was this option even considered? If not, it should have been. The offices of the DEA Regional Director and the ICE attaché are in the same building, less than one minute apart from each other. One way or another, they certainly would have accommodated a request like this. The biggest inconsistency is that there in fact had been a travel warning issued by the Ambassador to all agencies and offices in Mexico strictly prohibiting land travel within Mexico to the borde r or offices under states of high alert such as Nuevo Leon, San Luis, Coahuila, and Tamaulipas. The government sends these warnings t o all office heads within the country, requiring them to acknowledge and sign them. These office heads are then responsible for making their employees aware of such dangers. So how in the world did Victor's boss say he was not aware of any dangers in the area, when every single employee from a file clerk to Senior Executive Service employee and the Ambassador himself knew about the danger? Why was this man never held accountable for this horrendous decision by the Ambassador, his agency or the many politicians always looking for an axe to grind or a scalp to add to their long list of political hit jobs? There are too many unanswered questions. Questions that nobody wants to answer or downright refuse to answer.

To this day, thirteen years after the murder of Jaime Zapata and the attempted murder of Victor Avila, the answers to these questions remain unanswered, but somebody, somewhere has them and will probably take them to the grave with them. It is hard for me to fathom how someone in law enforcement could look at himself in the mirror knowing the answers to these questions and continue to live life as if nothing ever happened. Someday, however, they must answer those questions to a higher power when the time comes. And that time comes for all of us, eventually.

Chapter 15: The Worst Day

July 2011 was an extremely hot and humid month, even by Monterrey standards. Temperatures surpassed the 100-degree mark regularly. As a team, we pressed on with the Jaime Zapata investigation, trying to locate and apprehend the remnants of the Zetas involved in his death. We were experiencing a slowdown in the wake of the Jaime Zapata murder, but we remained focused on the prize of apprehending Zeta leader Miguel Trevino, also known as Z-40.

As human beings, we take refuge in the distraction amongst the chaos, and the city's two professional soccer teams, the Rayados and the Tigres of Monterrey, were set to face off on the weekend of July 23, 2011. The classic duel of the year, the "Clasico," as it is called, is comparable to the Dallas Cowboys vs the Washington Redskins on Thanksgiving Day, Yankees vs the Red Sox or the Celtics vs the Lakers. It was truly one of the classic rival matchups.

As one can imagine, the entire city goes into a frenzy whenever both teams clash, and this year was no different. In fact, it was even more intense because the Rayados were coming off a championship season and the Tigres were motivated to beat them to assert their place among Mexican soccer's elite teams. In Mexico, people are passionate about their families, soccer teams, food, music, politics, religion, and love, and this weekend set the stage for all those passions to meld in a grandiose celebration. The weekend was set up to be exciting, and everyone in the city, including us and the employees at the US Consulate, couldn't stop talking about the game. Our families were forced to leave the post in 2010, and we had united as a family ourselves. So, these festivities would be spent with our new de facto families at the consulate. After all, we were the only family we had left—our actual families were thousands of miles away.

Friday, July 22, 2011, started off as a normal day. Coming to work in the morning and being greeted with a "Buenos Dias jefe" by almost everyone was refreshing. Usually before entering the building, I would encounter the Consul General's, (CG and ranking State Department official), bodyguards, standing at the ready, dressed impeccably in their black suits and recently shined shoes next to the CG's armored Suburban, ready to whisk him away to his next meeting. These guys were sharp, highly trained individuals hand-picked specifically for the CGs protection detail from the Nuevo Leon State Police.

I enjoyed talking to the guards. They were a team of about eight. I started teasing them about how the Rayados were going to beat the Tigres soundly and that I didn't want to see them crying about it come Monday. We all laughed and enjoyed a friendly exchange of opinions on the outcome of the game. It was all in good fun. After all, laughter is the best medicine, especially during stressful times. The Zapata investigation had been an extremely tense time for all of us. So, the excitement and anticipation of the Clasico was a welcome distraction from the seemingly never-ending grind of tracking down t he Zetas.

The talk of the town and inside the US Consulate centered on what one's plans were for the weekend of the game, and predictions of who would win. Family barbecues, beer drinking while watching the game, listening to music and dancing after the game seemed to be the plan on everyone's list. On Monday, I had a scheduled trip to Washington, DC for in-service training, and I focused on planning my travel arrangements and ensuring that certain tasks in the office would be handled by my backup supervisor during my absence for a week. However, I was looking forward to enjoying the game with some of the Law Enforcement Team at my friend's restaurant, the Lil New York, because of its American menu of burgers, hotdogs, wings, and an assortment of cold beer. The CG was also traveling and had a scheduled departure that afternoon for a week-long vacation. It was a slow day, and the entire consulate work force hastily wrapped up loose ends before the big game weekend.

My boss, CG Nace Crawford, stopped by my office to say hello before heading out to the airport and we both wished each other a safe trip. We had a temporary duty agent from Corpus Christi, Texas who had been helping us out on the Zapata case, also leaving that day after having helped us out for three weeks. It was the perfect Federal Friday, everybody closing shop, preparing for and eager to start the weekend. The CG left for the airport at around 2:30 pm with his team of bodyguards and the rest of us prepared for the weekend ahead. Me and other members of the Law Enforcement Team were pondering where we were going to spend the rest of our Friday downing ice-cold Tecate Lights to ward off the effects of the summer heat and the immense stress we had been under. I, as the senior member of the Law Enforcement Team, had many suggestions, but I left it up to the rest of the team; as long as the beer was cold, it didn't matter to me.

Just as we were getting ready to leave the office at around 4:30pm, the Assistant Regional Security Officer (ARSO) came into my office with a look of horror and shock on his face. His face turned white as a sheet, practically hyperventilating, but he blurted out between deep breaths that unknown assailants had just attacked and killed two of CG Crawford's bodyguards in the neighboring town of Guadalupe, shortly after they left the US Consulate.

We couldn't believe what he was saying and confirmed it with him several times. Then we mobilized our personnel to respond to the scene and assist. But our superiors advised us to stand down in case the perpetrators were targeting Consulate personnel. We did not care and were prepared to face any hostility. But our superiors demanded again that we stand down, and we reluctantly complied. As we waited for additional information, we felt like caged lions, desperate to take action. We hurried back to our offices, the urgency in our actions matching the tension in the air. We retrieved our long guns, preparing for the possibility of being deployed or defending the Consulate.

Anxiety and despair consumed us as the specter of fear of the unknown permeated our psyche. Consulate employees still in the building at that hour were advised to stay in the building for safety reasons, adding to the anxiety, fear and psychosis. Considering all the violent actions the Zetas had taken on Consulate personnel, we could not be sure if this was a targeted act on our employees and we weren't about to take any chances. Personnel from the RSO's office went to the scene and confirmed the fact that it was Mr. Crawford's boys, our boys, our dear friends. The word spread throughout the entire consulate immediately. We'd gone from jovial brightness, expecting an exciting weekend with friends and family, to a sorrowful, obscure darkness in a matter of moments.

The Consulate suddenly felt like a funeral home—people crying and wailing in disbelief everywhere. The air was heavy with sorrow and an overwhelming sense of grief, affecting everyone in its presence. The entire Consulate community held Rolando Abrego Gonzalez and Arturo Zavala Ramos, the bodyguards, in high esteem and adoration. These two men, who were esteemed members of the State Police of Nuevo Leon, had faithfully served on the CG's protection detail for many years. We were left attempting to understand the motive behind the desire to harm them. Were they targeted because of their position as the CGs bodyguards? Was it a failed robbery attempt? Were they mistaken for Gulf Cartel members or Zetas? We all felt an extreme sense of helplessness, mixed with grief, anguish and despair. We were also pissed off and we needed answers.

The Protective Detail team left CG Crawford at the airport, and CG Crawford told them once they returned to the Consulate to go home since he would not need their services anymore. He told them to have a good weekend, enjoy the "Clasico" and he would see them upon his return. They all returned to the Consulate, where Abrego and Zavala changed out of their coat and tie uniforms and into their street clothes, then left together on a Suzuki motorcycle Zavala had purchased a few weeks prior. Ten minutes after leaving the Consulate, they were dead. Someone shot them from behind with an AK-47 rifle. The crime scene photos I reviewed were horrific; I will not describe them, but I will mention that Abrego took the worst of the attack and was killed instantly. Zavala was still alive when paramedics arrived on the scene but was dead on arrival at the hospital.

Coincidentally and luckily for us, CG Crawford's flight was delayed, so we contacted him and brought him back to the Consulate after informing him of the news. CG Crawford and the entire Law

Enforcement Team immediately reached out to law enforcement contacts, informants and other sources of information to try to piece together what happened and determine who was responsible. We found the events following this senseless act even more bizarre.

The State police of Nuevo Leon did not even send investigators to the scene until hours later. State police did not notify the family, rather they shockingly found out about the deaths through the media. CG Crawford was livid, but he tempered his sentiments so he could console the families of both officers. I will never forget the compassion and the empathy Mr. Crawford exhibited toward the Zavala and Abrego families and I will never forget the passion and unending resolve he displayed to the victims' superiors to exact justice on their behalf.

The response from the Nuevo Leon state government was practically non-existent. It seemed to us that they were annoyed that this incident had taken place. It was even more apparent that the deaths of their comrades seemed to be a nuisance when we attended their funerals the following day. In Mexico, if you die on Monday, you will be buried on Tuesday. There is no waiting for a family member to arrive from a far-off place. It is quick and final, and the funeral home wants its money immediately. On Saturday, July 23, what should have been a fun-filled family-oriented day became a living nightmare for the families of both men, including their consulate families.

CG Crawford, a few members of the Consulate community and I attended both funerals, the first of which was Zavala's. The US Law Enforcement members present at both services had our badges pinned to our lapels with black tape covering the badge, as is customary in the United States to honor a fallen comrade. But, the lack of police presence was surprising and disturbing. And when we finally arrived at Abrego's service, it was the same. No state police presence. No local police presence. No honor guard. No police caravan to the gravesite, Nothing. Zero.

At Abrego's funeral, I witnessed what to this day stands out to me as one of the most inspiring act of compassion I've seen. Abrego's wife was beyond consolation and the funeral home director kept pestering her and the family for payment or else the funeral home would not conduct the burial and it would be the family's responsibility to bury the body. CG Crawford was made aware of the funeral home director's demands and spoke to him in person, with me as a witness and another colleague as an interpreter. CG Crawford informed the funeral director of his identity and instructed him to cease any further contact with the family, while also inquiring about the remaining balance. He promptly paid with his personal credit card and informed the funeral director that the family and friends wanted to say goodbye to their loved one in peace. He also instructed the man to direct any further questions regarding the bill to CG Crawford. Finally, the family was able to say goodbye to their loved one in peace and we joined them in our farewells.

Abrego's funeral was a closed casket affair, unlike Zavala's. When it came time for the final Hail Marys before the casket was taken away, the family granted me, CG Crawford, and another colleague the privilege to approach the silver casket covered with white flowers and say our last goodbye to our friend, Abrego. The guy who I had joked with just the day before that the Rayados would prevail in the Clasico, who always greeted us with a smile and firm handshake, who loved American football as much as anyone, the guy who had been to my house, shared dinner with us and taken care of my children with the former CGs child. As we approached the casket, CG Crawford and I lay our hands on the casket as the family chanted the Hail Mary among tears and weeping. We both locked eyes and shook our heads as tears streamed uncontrollably from within the depths of our beating hearts and our languishing souls. No words needed to be exchanged between us. We were two heartbroken men who lost two brothers in an extremely illogical way bonded forever by their unfortunate and untimely deaths. I will never forget that moment. That moment is engraved in my mind, heart, and soul until the day I am called. Maybe then I will have the fortune and privilege of being reunited with Abrego and Zavala.

After both funerals, later that afternoon, I met up with one of my co-workers at the Lil New York for some drinks—I needed to get out of the house and not be alone. We were emotionally and mentally drained, in a zombielike trance, as we drank our beers. I had no emotion left. The suddenness of the tragedy had sucked it out of me. My heart felt like a blank piece of paper, withered under a barren, sun-beaten desert, then frozen by a gloomy gray sky. Attending two funerals in one day will do that to a man. The pain in our faces was so obvious, that even our friend Richard, the owner, asked us if we were alright. We drank our beers in silence, just staring out at the oblivion in the crystal blue sky in total disbelief, with tears occasionally streaming down our sleep deprived faces.

I personally, contemplated the fragility of life and the unpre-dictability with which it could be taken, shattering the sacred nucleus of the family forever. It seemed surreal to me that just yesterday I had shaken Abrego's hand and joked with him about the game, and today they buried him in the ground, never to return. Never to be seen by his family again, except in pictures. The same for Zavala. He was so proud of the motorcycle he had just purchased and wanted to show it to his friends at the Consulate. He was looking forward to getting home that day to prepare a barbeque in anticipation of the Clasico. Two young men, with young families and dreams for the future, gone in a flash. As much heartache as we felt at the loss of our dear friends, we knew it paled compared to what the families of both men felt. I could not even fathom the depth of pain and sorrow that the families were suffering through. Among the few words spoken between me and my coworker that afternoon, we made a vow to pursue the person or persons responsible for the murders of our friends relentlessly, no matter the cost.

For the next several weeks, the United States Law enforcement community hit the streets and interviewed every single informant, potential witness, including friends and neighbors we could find. We also put the word out on the street that there was a $50,000 reward in US Dollars being offered for any information leading to the arrest of the murderers. The irony here is that the reward was being offered by US Law Enforcement entities, not the Nuevo Leon State Police nor the State of Nuevo Leon. Our Marine commander was given the task of questioning every person they arrested or detained in hopes of obtaining information about our boys and catching a break.

We met with high-level state officials, including the Governor, the Attorney General, the Director of the Nuevo Leon command center, chiefs of police, all of whom promised us that an investigation was underway. However, their actions spoke to the contrary. For example, the command center in Nuevo Leon, called the C-5, provides useful information to help improve investigations. As such, the C-5 installs cameras in various thoroughfares in key cities of Nuevo Leon, such as Monterrey, San Nicolas, Santa Catarina, and Guadalupe, where our boys were killed. He promised to obtain and provide us with the video depicting the traffic activities from Avenida Morones Prieto on the exact date, and approximate hour, that our boys were killed. The commander ardently promised us we would receive his full cooperation in the matter and, with much fanfare, called one of his assistants and ordered him to find the video we wanted. It was an impressive show, but we never got the video. We called after about three days, but he was not available. The CG called him, and he said he was still working on it. A week later, he went on vacation. When he came back from vacation, he said he had too much work after vacation but would get back to us. We called the Attorney General, and he said he would look into it. We called the commander again, and he said his people were having trouble finding the exact video we had requested but were still on it. It was one excuse after another. Finally, we cornered him and asked him flat out if we were ever going to get the tape. Angrily and obviously annoyed by our presence, he made a complete 180-degree turn from his initial attitude and told us it was a State of Nuevo Leon matter and if we wanted the tape, we would have to make the appropriate diplomatic requests for the tapes. Whenever he was given the order, by either the Governor or Attorney General, he would, with much joy, give us the tapes we wante d.

We had hoped that they would set aside the effect of corruption for the sake of their own deceased colleagues. As much as we knew that corruption was pervasive in Nuevo Leon, he still held out a glimmer of hope that this case would be different. We hoped they would not sweep this under the rug and issue a trite statement of consolation, such as "they were killed as a result of mistaken identity," or "they must have been involved with organized crime and this was some sort of score that was settled." But that was exactly what was happening.

We should have known better.

As I mentioned in previous chapters, nobody cares as long as their mordida (bite) is not affected. The indifference with which the State of Nuevo Leon reacted to this tragedy astounded us. But we were undaunted. however, and refused to take no for an answer. DEA agents always try to find a solution to a seemingly impossible situation and, in this case, we took a highly unorthodox route to get what we wanted. In Mexico, the organization known as CISEN is the equivalent of the United States CIA and we had a highly reliable contact within the organization. We met with our contact and explained our situation. He readily agreed to help us out. Within a matter of a few days, we had the tape. We didn't ask questions about how or where he got the tape, but we knew we would owe him a huge favor in the future. We immediately reviewed the tape and, much to our surprise, the angle of the camera did not catch our boys. The tape was worthless. It made us wonder why the commander was so reluctant to let us have it when he knew there was nothing on it that would help us. The whole situation was just strange. We remained steadfast in our strategy with the Marines, diligently conducting interviews with every single person arrested, regardless of their position in the hierarchy. It would be short-lived, because, unbeknownst to us, we were about to get hit with another senseless tragedy.

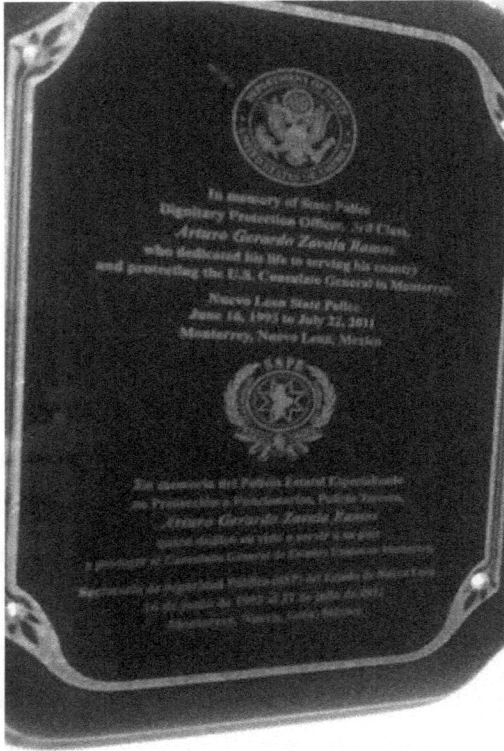

Plaque at the US Consulate Monterrey honoring Arturo Zavala Ramos.

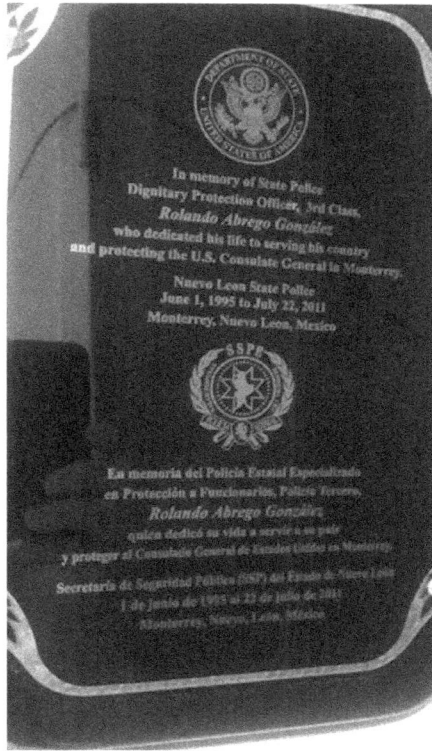

Plaque at the US Consulate Monterrey honoring Rolando Abrego Gonzalez.

**Abrego and Zavala with members of the US Consulate
security team.**

Chapter 16: Casino Royale

Marta Gonzalez-Cantu and Rosa Garza-Canales grew up together, went to school together, took vacations together and now that they were in their golden years, spent most of their days together. They had been best friends ever since they had cognitive usage of their minds, which nowadays seemed like an eternity to both women. They had dedicated their lives to their respective families, but now the kids had grown, raising families of their own, and their husbands had both passed on, leaving them a modest pension to live on. Now, the women were enjoying time to themselves, living each day to the fullest, in each other's company, like sisters, perhaps even closer than sisters. At the Sanborn's café in downtown Monterrey, they began each day with coffee and a light breakfast. Because of its old-fashioned diner style layout, they liked that particular Sanborn's, where they could sit back, enjoy their coffees, and reminisce about their younger days in the 1950s. They were both seventy-one in 2011, though the 1950s seemed like only yesterday to them—back when tranquility reigned in the city before crime and the Zetas imprisoned the entire country in terror and fear.

But they did not talk about such things. They preferred to talk about happy times, like when their parents would take them to the mountains in Arteaga Coahuila for Christmas vacation. Snow blanketed the ground as they played tag, running and laughing through

what seemed to be endless rows of apple orchards, occasionally stop-
ping to make snow angels in the plush ivory snow. After their afternoon in the orchards, they were treated to the most delightful and
toasty warm champurrado (a thick creamy Mexican hot chocolate)
or ponche de nuez (vanilla pecan punch, adorned with a cinnamon
stick) by a crackling fireplace, while their fathers roasted cabrito
(goat) in a smoldering oak firepit, oblivious to the snowflakes dancing
playfully in the spaces among the towering pine trees that surrounded their cabin. Their mothers, meanwhile, baked cookies, cakes and
made staggering amounts of buñuelos as desserts for friends and
family who visited. Those were wonderful memories, and they loved
reliving them at their daily breakfast before starting their day.

Today was Thursday—Casino Day—their favorite day of the
week, so they both ate lightly at breakfast so that they could conserve
their appetite for the buffet lunch at the casino later in the day. It
wasn't exactly Las Vegas, but the Casino Royale did a pretty good
job of providing a wide variety of entrees to choose from, and they
much preferred to save their appetites for the choices of regional
Mexican food, seafood, American food, sushi, Italian food, and the
best desserts in all of Mexico. Martita absolutely loved the roast bee
f and fluffy garlic mashed potatoes with a helping of asparagus, while
Rosita preferred the shrimp, sauteed in garlic butter, heaped on a
bed of steamed white rice and a side of mixed vegetables which they
both washed down with a glass of perfectly chilled Pinot Grigio.
Aside from winning a little money, the best part was indulging in the
heavenly mango cheesecake for dessert. They could hardly contain
themselves with the excitement and anticipation not only of maybe
winning a little money at the slots but for the meal itself. As soon
as they sat down to enjoy their meal, the thought of losing money

on the slots faded away, replaced by fond memories of happier times. They arrived at the casino, still buzzing from their light breakfast and the delightful conversation they had with their friends at the café.

While Martita and Rosita arrived at the Casino Royale, El Quemado was wrapping up instructions to his Zetas, the scent of a delicious lunch still lingering from his meal at the renowned El Gran Pastor restaurant, conveniently located just a few blocks away from their target. Crispy Cabrito with homemade corn tortillas and guacamole, washed down with some cold Tecate Light beers and Tequila served to quench their hunger and whatever fears they had before their mission.

"Has lo que tengas que hacer y te largas. No jotees y sobre todo que no te agarren, no la cagues! Quiero que entres y salgas lo mas pronto possible entendido?" ("You do what you have to do and leave! Don't linger around, don't get caught, don't fuck up! I want you in and out as fast as possible. Understood?")

The team leader, Mataperros (dog killer), nodded in agreement.

"Si jefe. No se preocupe. Todo saldra bien." (Yes, boss. Don't worry. Everything will be alright.)

El Quemado was known as "the Burned one" because he had burns over seventy percent of his body, mainly his face. The burns on his face gave him a reptilian like appearance which made his gaze creepy, unemotional, and intimidating, much like the gaze of a Komodo dragon. His burns were the consequences of an arson attempt that went bad. He had intended to extort a bar owner in Barrio Antiguo, which, no pun intended, backfired on him. The burns had been excruciating and the subsequent skin grafts and rehab were even worse. After the accident, his twisted and warped mind took a turn for the worse and he morphed into a more intense evil mind set than ever before. He hated everybody and everything and that is why Miguel Trevino chose him to be in a leadership position. He didn't give a shit about anyone or anything except his own disfigured face and body. Because he himself had suffered much more than any normal person could ever suffer, he had no mercy for anyone, and did not tolerate any excuses. He was angry at the world and everyone in it, at anyone who was normal or anyone who disagreed with him, except, of course, Miguel Trevino. He figured if I am going to be miserable, everyone else should be miserable, too.

Despite his twisted mindset, he took great pleasure in dressing lavishly, as if to make up for his grotesque appearance. He wore a black silk Armani shirt, black Gucci jeans, customized ostrich boots, a black 100X Presidente Stetson hat, gold chains hanging off his scarred neck, a diamond in his right ear, and a Blue faced Rolex Oyster Perpetual Submariner on his right wrist. He puffed on a cigarette as he squinted and stared lifelessly at Mataperros with that dragon look one last time before sending the team out on the mission. His tongue was slithering when he hissed out behind a cloud of smoke from the hole that was his putrid mouth.

"No la cagues pendejo" (Don't fuck up asshole).

Mataperros bit the inside of his lip, trying hard not to tremble at the zombie stare Quemado gave him, and simply nodded, and replied.

"Si jefe" (Yes boss).

He had no clue about the gravity of the crime he was about to commit. He just wanted to get out of this depraved and disgusting man's gaze as soon as possible before vomiting the cabrito he just ate at El Gran Pastor. And after making sure El Quemado was gone and satisfied with the plan, Mataperros took control of his team.

"Vamonos a la gasolinera cabrones. Pronto!" (Let's go to the gas station assholes! Quickly!)

Mataperros was following orders. He cared not about the consequences of his actions; more for the consequences of his inactions. If he did not do what El Quemado instructed, he was dead meat. Meat that would be tortured for hours on end by Quemado and possibly Miguel Trevino himself. So, he did what he was told and led his team of thirteen Zetas to a nearby Pemex gasoline station and topped off four fifty-liter portable gas canisters. In a convoy of four pickup trucks, they proceeded to the Casino Royale to complete the mission, just as Martita and Rosita sat down to enjoy their favorite meal on their favorite day at their favorite place.

The plan was simple: douse the place with gasoline, set the fire and get the hell out. Easy as pie, thought Mataperros as he pulled up to the entrance of the casino. Showtime! Although his heart was pumping a thousand beats a minute, everything seemed to slow down for Mataperros, as things do when adrenaline takes over.

He shouted to the rest of the team, "Orale cabrones pronto!" (Let's go assholes! Hurry!)

The Zeta, known as El Voltaje, jumped out of the pickup with two men armed with AK-47s and ran to the entrance of the casino, followed by three others with the gas canisters. As they took control of the casino, they violently smacked the hostess standing at the entrance with a .45 caliber Sig Sauer handgun. Security guards guarding the entrance were told to leave or die. Shocked customers watched in disbelief as the Zetas went to work, quickly dousing as much of the interior of the casino as possible, including a hot dog cart and a popcorn cart powered by propane gas. The combination immediately caused flames to shoot up almost to the roof of the casino.

"Ya se los llevo a la chingada cabrones!" (You are all going to hell, assholes!)

He shouted diabolically, simultaneously firing numerous rounds indiscriminately into the roof of the Casino. The shooting caused immediate chaos and a mad rush to the front exit by panicked customers playing bingo near the front entrance. Most of the terror-stricken crowd headed towards the back of the casino, hoping to escape the bullets. The powerful stench of gasoline permeated from the soaked carpet as the crowd, screaming frantically, dashed around, not knowing what to do or where to go or what was happening. As the flames intensified, El Voltaje made sure his fellow team members were safely out the door before tossing a Molotov cocktail onto the gasoline-soaked carpet. He watched as the cocktail exploded in a large whoosh, setting a fire that devoured the curtains, carpet, chairs, and everything else in sight. Enormous clouds of black smoke billowed from the front doors of the casino. Mataperros, Voltaje and the rest of the team took off. Mission accomplished in just under two minute s.

The focal point of the fire was at the entrance of the casino, impeding escape and trapping those who had not yet found a way out. For some unknown reason, someone had sealed the only designated emergency exit from the outside with a concrete wall, making it impossible to escape from within.

Martita and Rosita stared at each other paralyzed in horror as they watched the Zetas douse the casino, setting the hot dog cart and popcorn cart on fire. When the flames blazed to the roof of the building, they screamed in horror—just as Mataperros shot up the place.

"Santo Cielo! Que esta pasando? Vamonos de aqui Marta pronto!" (Holy heaven what is happening? Let's get out of here Martha quickly!)

Stunned, they watched in horror as Mataperros flung the Molotov cocktail onto the carpet in the casino. As the carpet and curtains became engulfed in a roaring flame, they could feel the intense heat on their faces. Lost and unsure of what to do, they found themselves amid a frenzied stampede, paralyzed with fear as they screamed for help that would never arrive. The screaming mad stampede overwhelmed them, and pushed them to the ground amidst the chaotic, panicked frenzy of the crowd. Glass shattered, flames crackled, and toxic black smoke quickly engulfed the casino; the roar of nerve-wracking screams intensified as the smoke and flames devoured the entire building. Something in Rosa's panic-stricken brain clicked, and she armed herself with courage, determined to survive the horrible nightmare in the infernal casino.

"Tenemos que hacer algo Martha vamonos a los banos! Ahi estaremos a salvo!!" (We must do something Martha. Let's go to the restrooms. We will be safe there.)

Martha did not respond but kept hysterically screaming for help as Rosa got to her feet and helped her up off the floor. She shook her hard hoping she would snap out of her shocked state of mind, then Rosa grabbed Martha by the arm and led her to where the bathrooms were located. The smoke severely hampered visibility:

her eyes burned, and her breath became laborious as she relied on her memory to guide her and Rosa to safety. The constant screams of the people trapped inside, also trying to survive, amped up her adrenaline, and survival instinct.

"Vamos Martha! Tenemos que salir de esto manita!" (Let's go Martha, we have to survive this sister.)

They finally made it to the bathrooms, only to find it packed with people also trying to survive the infernal flames and overpowering black smoke. Other victims were on their cell phones, frantically calling family members to come rescue them while others, already resigned to their fates, said their last goodbyes. Rosita and Martita both sat down in the bathroom's corner, exhausted. Their gazes met as smoke started billowing into the bathroom.

Rosita, with tears welling up in her eyes, said "Gracias por tu Amistad manita; eres mi hermana de siempre. te amo!" (Thank you for your friendship sister. You have been my sister forever. I love you.)

"Yo te quiero mas hermana! Vivimos una Buena vida. Si asi nos toco ir, vamonos con una oracion." (I love you more, sister. We have lived a good life. If this is the way we are going to go, then let us go with a prayer.)

They tightly clasped each other's hands, seeking solace in their shared prayer of the Hail Mary, their voices rising above the chaotic screams echoing through the blazing inferno. They embraced each other tightly as the smoke slowly overpowered their lungs. As the beautiful memories of their childhood danced in their minds like a Broadway musical, Martha and Rosa smiled at each other, their friendship forever sealed in an embrace of eternal love, even as the curtain fell and the lights went out.

Thursday, August 25, 2011, started out for me like any other day. We were searching for answers in the murders of Abrego and Zavala, hitting nothing but dead ends and receiving double talk from State officials at every turn. But we were not giving up. It was the least we could do for our fallen comrades. I was going home for a quick lunch when I noticed an immense cloud of black smoke off to the north, near Avenida Gonzalitos, one of the principal thoroughfares in Monterrey. The cloud was enormous, sinister, and menacingly foreboding. Flames were visible from the highway, which was several-miles away.

"That can't be good." I muttered to myself.

No sooner had I walked in the door when my phone rang. It was the RSO asking me to account for my employees and get back to him. There had been some sort of explosion in a casino off Avenida Gonzalitos close to where the state crime lab was located. He didn't know whether it was an accident or a planned attack. We had a close relationship with the Lab and wanted to make sure we were all accounted for. I immediately hit up my employees one by one, accounting for their safety, and reported back to RSO. He advised me to tell my employees if they were out of the office not to come back and just stay home. The Consulate was being closed down in case a follow-up attack was to be carried out on our building.

After this brief exchange, my phone lit up like a Christmas tree. The Marine commander called me to advise me that the Zetas had attacked the Casino Royale and that there were several people trapped inside. He asked me to advise him immediately if I received any intelligence on which Zeta was responsible. He said that he and his team were en route to the scene to assist with rescue attempts and that he would report on the results as soon as he could.

I immediately advised my boss in Mexico City that the Zetas had perpetrated an explosion of some type in a heavy transit zone in Monterrey, but that all our employees were safe and accounted for. Friends and contacts started calling me, scared and wanting to know what was happening and whether it was safe to be out on the street. There were many rumors flying around, from the explosion being caused by a car bomb to an electrical fault in the wiring. Chaos and terror gripped the city for the rest of the day, into the night—unfortunately, it would rule the city for the next several days, as desperate, terrified family members of people trapped inside waited for news regarding their loved ones.

I visited my friend's restaurant, the Lil New York, which was the same place where my colleague and I had met after the killings of Zavala and Abrego. It had become a meeting place, or second office, for me, my colleagues, and friends. Information came slowly and in bits and pieces, and what we got was tragic. By 9 PM, the death toll was up to forty and the rescue teams were still not through searching. The following day, the death toll had risen to sixty-one. The fear and terror that reigned over the city gave way to a tremendous sense of grief and sorrow. Most of the victims were elderly ladies who enjoyed playing bingo or the slot machines. It was a senseless act perpetrated by the Zetas. We did not understand what the Zetas stood to gain by committing such a cowardly act. For us, it was another hard-hitting tragedy. People described it as the worst mass murder in the history of Mexico. It was only a month after Zavala and Abrego had been killed, and we were still grieving for them.

Now, this tragedy added to the depths of our sorrow.

Despite the challenging circumstances, we painstakingly pieced together the details of that day. Witnesses stated that at approximately

3:50 PM, which is the height of the lunch hour in Mexico, a group of about twelve armed men, in four different vehicles, entered the casino shouting profanities, shooting rounds into the roof of the building and ordering people to leave. Simultaneously, other members of the group began pouring three large containers, each holding around 200 liters of gasoline, onto the entrance of the casino, the carpet, and a few of the slot machines. Some fortunate people instantly ran out of the building, but others ran towards the back of the casino to take cover, fearing that they would be shot to death. At some point, the group ignited the gasoline-soaked casino, which erupted into a blazing inferno within seconds. It took the group only about 2 minutes to unleash terror and bedlam on the unsuspecting victims.

The victims who ran towards the back of the casino tried to escape through the back door emergency exits, but the doors had been sealed shut, for reasons still unknown to this day, from the outside by a concrete wall, leaving them trapped. Other victims hid in the bathrooms and used their cell phones to call out to authorities and loved ones to report what was happening. The fire consumed the place in seconds and the smoke turned an otherwise well-lit place into an infernal, pitch-black darkness. There was no way out for the victims. Many of the victims made calls to their loved ones bidding them farewell, often staying on the line until the smoke consumed them and they could talk no more.

According to one witness, she received a phone call from her mother and could hear the desperate cries of the trapped victims in the background. Rescuers could not enter the casino because of the thickness of the smoke and intensity of the fire. With minimum equipment at their disposal, they tried to break through the concrete walls with pickaxes and sledgehammers as they simultaneously tried to douse the fire. A crew working construction nearby knocked down a wall of the casino with a bulldozer, but it was too late to rescue anyone. Smoke inhalation caused the death of most of the victims, but many victims died from burns.

The entire country grieved on that humid summer day, but nothing could surpass the anguish, sorrow, or torment that the citizens of Monterrey and the state of Nuevo Leon suffered on that day. There are no words in any language known to man capable of describing the desperation and terror that the victims suffered at the hands of the Zetas during their last moments on this earth. President Felipe Calderon described the tragedy as an "act of terrorism" and declared three days of national mourning. President Obama described the tragedy as "brutal and reprehensible." Leaders from all over the world expressed their solidarity with the people of Monterrey and Mexico.

None of these statements by world leaders meant much to the victims' families. Their loved ones were gone forever. No amount of sympathy could compensate for the losses they suffered in such a senseless act. To this day, there is no monument to honor the lives of the victims who died in that cowardly and senseless attack. Just another incident in Mexico, swept under the rug by indifference, politics and passaging time. However, the amount of political pressure the tragedy brought to the Governor was so intense that the State police actually did their jobs. Within weeks El Voltaje was in custody and quickly ratted out the other members of his crew. El Mataperros was killed as he tried to shoot it out with the police trying to avoid capture.

As in past transgressions, when his underlings acted with complete disregard for his authority, Trevino was enraged and breathing fire. Trevino was practically frothing at the mouth when he gave the order to every Zeta member to find El Quemado and bring him back alive, so he could take the pleasure of dealing out a slow, painful, and methodical torture. He would never get the opportunity or satisfaction. El Quemado went into hiding and used every bit of the skill set he had learned from his days in the Mexican Special forces to avoid Trevino's wrath.

But Trevino and the Zetas hitmen were not his only worry. President Calderon ordered that his capture be considered the highest priority in the country, so every entity in the country—SEDENA, SEMAR, the Federal Police, and the State Police of Nuevo Leon—wanted him, dead or alive. He took his chances, but his odds of survival were slight to none. Luck does not last forever, no matter how skilled you are. On April 5, 2012, while on patrol in the outskirts of Nuevo Laredo on the highway to Piedras Negras Coahuila, SEDENA encountered a convoy of vehicles occupied by heavily armed men, who immediately engaged the soldiers in an intense firefight that ended the lives of four of the suspects. According to sources in SEDENA, one individual was difficult to identify because of the scar tissue from severe burns to his face, body and extremities, the handgun on the body of this individual had the inscription "Quemado" across the still hot and smoking barrel of the silver-plated gun. They finally put an end to El Quemado's demonic misery, ensuring he would never inflict any suffering on innocent lives again.

First responders at the scene of Casino Royale fire.
(Photo courtesy of Grupo Reforma / El Norte)

Chapter 17: Nowhere to Run

T revino was the most feared man in Mexico, leader of the most feared criminal organization in North America. But he was tired. He was tired of running and the US Government and Government of Mexico knew it. He was tired of always looking over his shoulder. He was tired of sleeping on the ground on some desolate ranch with spiders, ants, snakes and only the mesquite trees and cacti to keep him company. He longed for a cool bed with a comfortable mattress, so he could sleep comfortably and soundly for more than two hours at a time. What he yearned for was the simple things: the aroma of breakfast wafting from the kitchen, the enticing scent of machacado con huevo, accompanied by warm, homemade flour tortillas and a steaming cup of robust Chiapas coffee. He had more money than he could spend and could easily buy what he wanted, but he could not enjoy it with anyone. He was unable to share a home-cooked meal with his family or girlfriend, or take his girlfriend out for a fancy dinner, or enjoy a movie night with her. Family vacations were completely off the table. Other than his brother, he trusted no one. He could not do much of anything except keep an eye out for the enemy. The constant life on the run stripped away any joy or satisfaction he once found in life's simplest pleasures. He w as exhausted.

The challenges of being on the run are magnified when it seems like every person you encounter is after you. In his case, a myriad of law enforcement agencies were on the hunt for Miguel Trevino, including the Federal Police, Mexican Army, Mexican marines, DEA, FBI, ICE, ATF, and the US Marshalls. Not to mention the Gulf Cartel, Sinaloa Cartel, and even some of his own Zetas were also seeking to apprehend him. He was the most wanted man in Mexico, and the burden was weighing heavily on him. One of our sources told us that Trevino once said that one second for him was like a minute for anyone else, one minute for him was like an hour for anyone else, and one hour for him was like a whole day for anyone else. Time was precious to him, because he knew that at any moment, the clock could stop ticking for him, one of his cartel rivals or the Mexican military, could put a stop to the hourglass of his life.

We had no doubt that Trevino, just like the majority of the other Zeta leaders, would not give up easily. Trevino brought all his problems on himself, first with the grenade incident at the US Consulate, then the near capture of Lazcano in November 2008, next came the attack on the ICE agents in San Luis Potosi, followed up by the burning of the Casino Royale in Monterrey.

When Trevino gave the order to Canicon to launch a grenade attack on the US Consulate, he woke up the sleeping giant that is the United States government's presence in Mexico, dormant since the 1985 kidnapping of Special Agent Enrique Camarena. Every federal agency placed themselves on high alert and made Trevino their priority target. This incident truly marked the beginning of the end for the entire Zetas organization because the US government has a long memory and would never let that incident slide. At the time, the Zetas, who were still considered the enforcement arm of the Gulf

Cartel, had some high-ranking members of the Gulf Cartel who were not happy with Trevino for making the decision to attack the US Consulate. They knew it would bring never-ending heat to the organization. This decision by Trevino, though not the primary cause, was part of the reason for the eventual fracture and war between the Gulf cartel and the Zetas in 2010.

The GOPES operation targeting Heriberto Lazcano in San Luis, Potosi shook Lazcano to his core, leaving him a nervous wreck and extremely paranoic, so much so that he went into seclusion and ceded most of the Zeta leadership to Trevino. This transfer of power caused a significant amount of suspicion among Zeta members, some of whom believed Trevino sold Lazcano out to the GOPES for his own personal gain. Lazcano was never the same after the GOPES operation. In October 2012, SEMAR engaged in a shootout with Lazcano in Progreso, Coahuila, resulting in his death. Lazcano's death cast even more doubt on Trevino among Zeta members who again strongly believed Trevino had betrayed Lazcano to SEMAR, leaving him as the de facto leader of the Zetas. What made Lazcano's death even more suspicious was the fact that a group of heavily armed men stormed the funeral home where he was taken and stole his body, and it was never found or seen again. To this day, no one knows why or where the body ended up, except maybe for Trevino himself. Lazcano wished to be buried in his hometown of Pachuca Hidalgo. He certainly did not want to disposed of in Coahuila.

The attack on ICE agents Jaime Zapata and Victor Avila, which resulted in agent Zapata's death, though not ordered by Trevino, was still a critical factor in the US Governments efforts to apprehend Trevino. The Zetas carried out the attack, therefore, as their leader, he was responsible. The US Government will never forgive organized crime for murdering one of its agents.

The attack on the Casino Royale, wherein approximately 60 innocent victims perished, was unforgiveable in the eyes of then President Felipe Calderon. Days after the attack, he met with the leaders of SEMAR and SEDENA and ordered them to do whatever it took to capture Trevino. Even though Trevino did not give the order, as the leader of the Zetas, he was responsible in the eyes of the Mexican government.

Everyone was after him. He was running out of allies and places to hide.

Upon realizing he was under suspicion by members of his own organization, Trevino retreated and limited his circle of security to just three or four trusted individuals. He changed cell phones daily, sent orders through his brother Omar, and avoided contact with any members of the organization. He was a hunted man.

The US State Department offered a five-million-dollar reward for information leading to his arrest, and the Government of Mexico offered a reward of thirty million pesos (2.3 million USD), a tempting reward for anyone in his organization who wanted to collect that money and Trevino knew it. He hardly ever slept and when he could, he slept on the ground in remote ranch lands.

In April 2013, a close associate of our office was kidnapped and murdered in Monterrey, causing us to shift our focus to the criminal group responsible for his death. Our office passed the torch on the Trevino investigation to the US Marshalls. After all, the United States indicted Trevino in both New York City and Washington DC, and he became a fugitive from justice. The US Marshalls' specialty is tracking down fugitives, so our office entrusted them with Trevino.

There was no investigation left for us to conduct, anyway. We had done what we could and moved on to more pressing matters. It was only a matter of time before someone either sold him out to collect the reward money or killed him. In the best-case scenario, SEMAR would capture him and extradite him to the United States for trial in either New York or Washington, DC.

In July 2013, my US Marshall counterpart advised me they were enthused about a signal on a phone possibly being used by Trevino. They felt encouraged because the signal would go off during the day and power up in the early morning hours, which was consistent with Trevino's pattern of life. On July 15, 2013, the US Marshalls teamed up with SEMAR to track down the signal. The signal led them to a desolate road in Anahuac, Nuevo Leon, where a pickup truck occupied by three individuals traveled south. One of those individuals was the holder of the phone. SEMAR, using a Blackhawk helicopter, landed the chopper in the middle of the highway to impede the truck's movement. One individual who had run from the truck was later apprehended by SEMAR. That individual turned out to be the most feared man in Mexico, Miguel Trevino Morales.

The SEMAR personnel discovered that the truck was filled with an assortment of high-powered weapons, none of which were utilized by Trevino or his bodyguards, thankfully. They also found a duffle bag stuffed with hundred-dollar bills, approximately $2 million dollars, which he promptly offered to SEMAR in exchange for his freedom. SEMAR had their orders from President Calderon, and they would not let him go under any circumstances. The hunt was over. His capture ended the bloodiest era ever to occur in Mexico.

In all my years as a DEA agent, I have never encountered someone with such blatant disregard for human life as Trevino. The only person I can think of that could be worse is probably Pablo Escobar. This was a man who ordered the entire town of Allende, Coahuila, to be wiped out, men, women and children, because he suspected someone of snitching on him. This is besides the countless murders he and his organization committed over several years causing anguish and pain to so many people within the country and leaving countless families to live with the void and sorrow created by their loved one's violent passing at the hands of this organization. We were relieved that he was in custody and that the reign of terror that he oversaw and undertook on the entire country was finally over.

Epilogue

At my farewell party, surrounded by my closest friends in Monterrey, my boss, the Consul General gave a speech, which he ended by saying that our mission was to make a difference in people's lives. "You, Leo, have definitely made a difference in people's lives, not only in Monterrey, but in all of Mexico."

I struggled to maintain my composure when he uttered those words because my mind immediately drifted to the people I failed, such as Abrego, Zavala, Jaime Zapata, and all their respective families with whom I did not and could not make a difference. I did the best I could within my power to help them and other people in need. But that does not bring peace to my soul.

They are gone forever, and their families must live with that horrific void and solace in their lives forever.

My team and I did our absolute best in every endeavor, no matter how big or small. I know it and God knows it. That is good enough for me. I have long since retired and I feel a certain sense of tranquility whenever I return to the coastal city of South Padre Island, where my mother used to bring me and my siblings to escape the pressures of life in the 1970s. After all the years that have passed in my life, this place still serves as a refuge for me and my soul. The palm trees swaying against the fresh coastal breeze, and the gently lapping waves of the warm Gulf waters soothe the scars in my soul as I walk barefoot on the placid shore, with my wife and precious granddaughter.

My granddaughter displays her pure innocence in her joyous laughter as she splashes around in the sun-gilded waves, with seagulls cackling in the background, just like me and my siblings did when we were her age. Precious, tranquil moments that I will treasure forever, a stark and welcome contrast to my time in Monterrey. She does not know what evil is, nor do I want her to know, ever. I want to see her like this forever, happy, blissful, and at peace. For now, Monterrey, the Zetas, the Gulf Cartel, the Beltran Leyva organization and all the evil demons that we dealt with fall deep into the recesses of my mind, as if they were all part of a horrific ancient dream.

But they are not. And sometimes, when I least expect it, the dreams come haunting me, jumping out of the shadows of my unconscious mind to remind me of their ubiquitous existence, refusing to be forgotten. This is my motivation for writing this book. Not for the demonic souls we encountered, but to ensure that the efforts and relentless dedication to duty by SEDENA, SEMAR, Federal Police, DEA, US Marshalls, FBI, ICE, and ATF are never forgotten.

As I take my beachside walk, hand in hand with my wife and granddaughter, watching God's artistic masterpiece of purple, blue, white, orange, and pink sunset, I can truly say with sincerity that I have no regrets and I silently quote,

2 Timothy 4:7; I have fought the good fight. I have finished the race, and I have kept the faith.

Leo Silva at the US Consulate Monterrey. (Circa July 2014)

All About the Author

Leonardo "Leo" Silva is a native of Brownsville, TX, a charming seaside city on the border. He is a 1982 graduate of Homer Hanna High School and received a Bachelor of Arts degree in Literature from The University of Texas-Brownsville in 1985. He served as a Special Agent/ Supervisory Special Agent with the United States Drug Enforcement Administration from 1987 to 2015. During his career, he was assigned to offices along the Southwest border, Guadalajara, Jalisco and Monterrey Nuevo Leon, Mexico. "Reign of Terror" is based on his experiences in Mexico and is his first True Crime novel.

www.ingramcontent.com/pod-product-compliance
Lightning Source LLC
Chambersburg PA
CBHW030821090426
42737CB00009B/817